The Life of

Tolka

Published By

www.poetryworld.org

The Life of Tolka

Written by Nitin Chopra & Niveditha Preeth

Published by: Poetry World Org.

Publisher's Address: Haryana

Printed under PWO in India

Edition: I (2023)

ISBN (Paperback) – 9789392507052

Book Design by POETRY WORLD

POETRY WORLD ORG 2023

The Life of Tolka

Authors

Dr. Nitin Chopra

Dr. Niveditha Preeth

tale of narrow escape from the merciless shelling and firing bullets. A traumatic nightmare of death and destruction that haunts every survived soul till their last breath.

To the innocent souls lost and the surviving brave hearts

To every writer reading this,

Thank you for choosing this book. You know what? I can feel you. I understand your emotions completely!

To craft a line that records itself into the pages of history, a writer often surrenders fragments of their own life, capturing what the world experiences but struggles to articulate, immortalizing the pain within their words. They sacrifice their essence to compose melodies that resonate with the cosmos, a sacrifice that sometimes feels like it takes to destroy one's life to write one line that he as a writer will be remembered for. Amidst whispers of disbelief, some claim I fail to comprehend the dialect of love. To them, I offer an insight: love is a shade woven from infinite languages.

Love's vocabulary is as diverse as the souls that encounter it. Perhaps I spoke a dialect unfamiliar to those who crossed my path, leading them to question its authenticity. And so, I persist, penning my narrative in a language only my heart can truly decipher. To love and to lose is a universal truth, but for men, it's often an unspoken pain. Behind every strong man, there's a story of love that he carries silently, tears unshed are not tears avoided; they are tears that carve hidden rivers of sorrow within. A man's silence can echo louder than his words, especially when it conceals the depths of his heartache.

A writer's silence is the loudest scream; it's the unwritten chapters of their life that echo in the emptiness of their soul. In the darkest corners of a writer's heart, you'll find the stories that never made it to the page, the ones too painful to share but too profound to forget. When you break a writer's heart, you're not just shattering their emotions; you're crushing their soul. To heal, they scream, but not with vocal cords—they scream through their words, a chorus of anguish that echoes in the silence of their solitude.

When you break a writer's heart, you fracture the universe of their imagination, leaving constellations of shattered dreams. Their capacity to feel pain surpasses the ordinary, and it's this depth that empowers them to take on the sacred responsibility of articulating the collective pain of humanity. Through the window of imagination, we glimpse worlds we can never touch, and sometimes, the view is more heart-wrenching than the closed doors we've left behind. Life may offer different souls to share joy with, but it is the one person with whom you share commitment that anchors you amidst the chaotic tides of existence. When this commitment falters, it sends shockwaves through the very core of your being, threatening the love that binds you.

Emotions are the ink, and life is the canvas; writers craft masterpieces of heartache and hope, painting the human experience with words. He promised to be their hero, even when the world forgot to be his. A man's strength isn't measured by his silence, but by the tears he holds back, for he's a prisoner of his own strength, sentenced to a lifetime of silent suffering. He vowed to be the protector, but who protects the guardian when darkness consumes his soul? His tears are a silent testament to the battles he fights within himself.

PROLOGUE

"We are at all times unconscious prophets."

— Charles Spurgeon

Chaos… Blood… Death…

The room was full of dead bodies, arms, and legs severed and lying randomly one above the other while some bodies were without their heads. Blood was spilt everywhere, sprayed on the walls and the floor, and was dripping from the roofs too. I was in the middle of the room, hands covered in blood and clothes soaked wet - a mixture of sweat and blood. Scared out of my wits, I was rooted to the spot, heart drumming loud and fast. My breathing was ragged, and I felt suffocated. The air smelled of death. My chest was getting heavy while the vision in front of my eyes started to blur.

Not able to stand there any longer, my legs trembled as I turned towards the window and jumped out of it, breaking the glass. The pain due to the shards of glass that pierced my body was nothing compared to the terror that was creating havoc in my mind. Life presents doors that slam shut, both figuratively and literally, forcing them to peer longingly through windows of their imagination. But what if this window offers no escape, only a view into a world they can never physically inhabit? My racing heart didn't calm down and the grim aura seemed to follow. I looked around and found myself standing in front of the park where I went for a walk yesterday. Through my blurry eyes, I saw numerous white figures near the trees. I inched closer and rubbed my eyes, steadying myself to take a better look.

When my eyes focused, dread and horror hit me hard. The whole park was filled with dead bodies much worse than the room I was in. The kids who had been smiling happily during the day and their parents who had a warm smile, were among the dead, lying on the ground in a pool of blood, eyes wide open, revealing the horror they went through right before their souls departed. The elderly couple's bodies were charred as they were hugging each other on the same bench where I last saw them. The young couple's faces were covered in smoke, dust, mud, and blood, their hands tightly interlocked with each other a few feet away from their bodies.

Breathless, I ran faster only to face a more agonising sight. In a garden full of trees, there were bodies of the dead wrapped in pure white muslin cloth, hanging from the branches of the trees. It seemed like the trees bore dead bodies on each branch instead of ripened fruits or bright flowers. The green grass was fully covered in blood; both dried and fresh and appeared as a red bed of grass. Blood drops were dripping from the bodies hanging from the ropes tied to the trees and droplets of blood rained from the sky. My heart was racing like a horse and my breaths were getting shallow and deep.

I jolted awake, sweating profusely. My pillow was wet with tears and sweat. The nightmare had been so horrifying that I couldn't bat an eyelid through the night. I walked around the house restlessly, my heart still drumming in horror and fear. I checked the door locks and windows and found them secure. My eyes darted towards the walls, wanting to assure myself. The walls, floors, and ceiling were clean as before, devoid of blood, while the air was cool in the air-conditioned room without the smoky rotten metallic smell.

Tears were flowing down at random intervals out of panic and grief as the vision resurfaced in front of my eyes uninvited. I was feeling so edgy that I was running around the house like a madman, thinking of something, anything, to divert my thoughts. Out of desperation, I started cleaning the house in an attempt to remove the traces of the horrifying nightmare from my mind. However, I was still not able to keep my anxiety in check. So, I quickly went out of the house to inhale the fresh air, as everything I did to calm my racing mind and heart was of no use. At times, the prophecy of dreams can be too shattering to accept.

It was day-break, and the sun had peeked out of its slumber. I strolled around the area, avoiding the park. People were rushing for work and tourists were walking around in awe, admiring the beauty, and clicking selfies.

Though the city bustled with activity, it was calm and serene, unlike the chaos in my dream. My dreams and intuitions were usually potent and the probability of them coming true was higher. So, I fervently hoped and prayed that this time, it wouldn't come true. I hoarded a few groceries, gathered a few important necessities and spent the rest of the day playing with my cat and dog.

The night grew monstrously dark, more so as I remembered the previous night's events. Fright still gripped my heart as I went to sleep, wishing for a fresh day to start. Alas! I only realised how wrong I was to wish and hope, when I was startled awake, yet again, but this time, by a massive deafening boom followed by harsh tremors.

CHAPTER – 1

"War is neither glamorous nor attractive. It is monstrous. Its very nature is one of tragedy and suffering."

— Dalai Lama

КИЇВ
KYIV
Kyiv Tv Tower, Dorohozhychi (Kyiv
СТАЛО
BEFORE
СТАЛО
AFTER

The subconscious mind is powerful and can gauge what the brain refutes, either out of unwillingness or because of logic. However, more often than not, the subconscious is correct.

The clock pointed its needles at four-thirty early in the morning. As I sat up with a jolt, I wondered if it was an earthquake. Before I could wrap my mind around what was happening or think about the reason, a second boom was heard. This time, it was much closer and louder than the first.

Moments later, when I peeped out of the window, I saw clouds of alternating light and dark grey smoke, the shape of a mushroom cloud, reaching the sky, which turned darker and larger as seconds ticked by. Before I could overcome that shock and my half-asleep state, a third boom resonated a few metres from my apartment. In the silence of the night, the noise was ear-piercing and clear.

My heart pounded in fear, and the shivers in my body mirrored the tremors of the building. Glasses all around the house were trembling and quivering violently. To my horror, I even noticed minor cracks starting to form at the corners of the building walls. Hell! I wasn't sure about what was happening. Maybe I had a hunch, but my heart refused to acknowledge it. I still believed that no one would have the heart to disrupt the peace and beauty of this place. Like a fool, I had ignored the alarming bells that rang in my head, which made me realise that my nightmares were coming true. My panicked heart's beat raised an octave as I heard many aircraft flying over the sky, followed by blaring sirens of ambulances, fire engines, and police vans.

In the next few seconds, loud alarm warnings echoed throughout the city. It was a confirmation of my worst fears coming true. In a moment, my mobile started displaying calls and messages from my family and friends. Right now, my life was hanging by a thread while my priorities were swaying on both sides of the scale, as I didn't know whether to attend the calls and assure them about my well-being or to run and hide in the safety shelters. I picked up the call from my parents, simultaneously changing my shorts and picking up my power bank, headphones, and whatever else I could lay my hands on. Though it was difficult, I spoke as if everything was fine and that I wasn't aware of what was happening in Kyiv.

My father was advising me to stay safe and informed me about the bombing in Kyiv by the Russians. I assured them that the situation in the place I stayed was calm and normal, while the sirens on the streets proved my blatant lie. In the background, I heard my mom's sobs and her constant chanting of prayers from behind my father. In between the chants, she was yelling at my father to force me to return to India. She was cursing herself for letting me go far away from her in the first place. Convincing them about my safety, I disconnected the call and rushed to the nearby subway station, Demiivska, where people had gathered for shelter.

The crowd was full of fear-filled faces, making me wince, as the incident had robbed the peace of the once calm and happy people. The air of grief was too much to bear. Though everyone tried their best to be strong, their eyes and pale faces gave away their fears. We hoped the situation would end in a day, and we would be able to go back to our normal lives. Being clueless about which move will catapult us towards danger, we stay put in the underground shelter, not daring to move even an inch. I was trying to gather my strength and calm down.

Life is unpredictable, and I am a living testimonial of that. It loves pulling me out of my comfort zone and throwing me into unexpected situations. It seems to be a never-ending test, and I'm sure it always chooses me first to be tested in case of complex struggles. If there is one thing that I hate the most, it is being unprepared. However, that was the case with me of late.

My dreams and achievements were like a slip between the cup and the lip. If I were to personify life, it would be the grumpy-looking, wrinkled-skinned, big-eyed man, wearing thick round shell-frame glasses, carrying a long wooden stick in his hand to strike my butt, whenever I slowed down in the race.

Just a few days back, life had looked so promising to me. When one thinks that everything is going as per plan, life decides to surprise with unforeseeable circumstances, shaking the very foundation of the being. I was exhausted, thinking about the multitude paralogies that could be possible in the current situation. At one point, I closed my eyes and rested my head against the wall, wanting to cut off from the petrifying circumstances and get lost in the happy memories of my trip.

CHAPTER 2

"Travel expands the mind and fills the gap."

— *Sheda Savage*

Quarantine — a word I'm sure the entire world dreads today. It'd take many years for people to normalise after the impact it had on their lives. And I'm no exception. After many months of lockdown and quarantine, I stepped outside to see the world. I had to unwind my mind and reset my life. Not sure where to fly, I chose Belgrade, Serbia, the nearest destination from Kyiv, Ukraine. I was excited to feel the fresh air and visit a new place despite the COVID restrictions that were still being followed. The itinerary for my entire trip was all set.

The flight from Kyiv to Belgrade was short and smooth. After landing, I went directly to my hotel to unload my luggage and freshen up. I dressed up in one of my favourite shirts and walked to the city centre. My first destination was Kneza Mihaila, a simple yet beautifully adorned pedestrian street and shopping zone at the city's centre. It's said to have the oldest and the most valuable landmarks. I walked at a leisurely pace, lost in the beauty of the vintage buildings and mansions built in the 1870s. Over the years, they evolved into shopping zones, but I appreciated how the buildings were still preserved and carried their historical importance.

Man-made pillars that extended to arches welcomed the pedestrians to the shopping zone. Strings of lights stretched from the entrance to a noticeable distance, adorning the tunnels. It was like walking in a fantasy land, illuminated with fairy lights. The word enchanting won't do justice to the atmosphere I experienced at that time. The street buzzed with people rejoicing their time together. The pavements were neat, and the grass was well-maintained. Golden light arches were constructed in many places that added charm to the silence. I walked ahead in a dazed state, as my eyes kept darting around, taking in the charming atmosphere while excitement bubbled inside me.

I must have been a few miles away when I spotted a small clearing at the junction of two roads where a simple Wi-Fi and water terminal were built. While roaming around, I lost sense of time. However, as soon as I saw the water, I realised how thirsty I was! Like a kid who runs towards a chocolate counter, I sprinted towards the terminal and drank some water. The crystal-clear water quenched my thirst. I even clicked a few pictures of the place to retain the wonderful memory, shopped for a few souvenirs, and went back to my hotel.

The next day's journey began from the Belgrade fortress. It is officially declared as the 'Monument of Culture' and is under the protection of the Republic of Serbia. The beauty and the grandeur of the place are such that it is one of the most frequently visited places by tourists. They occasionally conduct open-air concerts too, but my time of visit wasn't appropriate to witness one. The Kalemegdan Park covers a large area and the spectacular view of the confluence of the Sava and Danube rivers took my breath away.

I walked between the two fort pillars, marvelling at the sheer brilliance of the people during those times, when there was no trace of the advanced technology that we take for granted today. There were a lot of solo travellers like me as well as people visiting in groups.

Travelling to bygone places is a refreshing experience, as if they have a story to tell. I felt I could get lost for hours, gazing at the sculptures, monuments and artefacts, transporting in time and losing myself in that era.

I noticed a girl around my age, walking behind me. On observing closely, she looked like a native to me. She saw me gazing at the fort with awe and smiled. "Majestic, isn't it?"

I smiled back. "Yeah, it is. Do you mind suggesting some good places to visit while I'm here?"

"Novi Sad, Nikola Tesla Museum, Palace Iron Man, and Name of the Mary Catholic Church are some notable and must-visit places." I was mentally making a note of the places mentioned, when she added, "Hope you have a wonderful time."

I thanked her and proceeded towards the museum first, which caught my attention. It was the final resting place of Nikola Tesla, and this museum was built in his honour. My eyes widened in awe at the sight of each of his inventions. There were many books, journals, and original documents on the display. The organisers had arranged a small demonstration for the tourists, and I was glad to take part.

After having a memorable time at the fortress, I still had the evening to myself and headed to see the Monument of Stefan Nemanja, which is another prominent landmark of Belgrade. As I approached the monument, I felt overwhelmed by the sheer size and felt it was an opt ode to the Nemanjic dynasty that contributed so much to the advancement of the people. The day's excursion made me more excited to explore the other historical sites in the days to follow.

The visit to Avala Tower, a tall telecommunication tower situated on Mount Avala, was another one-of-a-kind experience. Though there was an option of travelling by tram or taxi, I opted to climb. It was a half-an-hour's climb on the inclined path of the mountain, which elevated the entire experience. After reaching the mountain top, I rested for a bit and then took a lift to the top of the tower. When I reached there, I was spellbound as the entire city and the nearby areas were visible from up there, which was a sight to sore eyes. I fell in love at first sight. The picturesque view was so breathtaking that it brought goosebumps to my skin while I inhaled fresh air into my lungs. The only thought I had then was, 'If this is how love feels, I'd gladly fall in love every day.'

As per the flyer, in 1999, when Serbia was a part of the Federal Republic of Yugoslavia, this tower fell prey to the NATO bombing of Yugoslavia. The mere thought of destruction made me wince, and I was glad that the structure had been resurrected.

Destruction can be devastating. The ones who do not stumble despite major pitfalls and have the courage to stand up once again, always win.

The next day, I visited Novi Sad, Serbia's second-largest city. Located on the banks of the Danube River, I was enchanted by the peaceful city and didn't realise where time flew by, as I explored the city on foot for a couple of hours. In the city, I visited the Name of Mary Catholic Church. The neo-gothic arches and the stained glasses had a story to tell of their own, while I revelled in the positive vibes of the place.

Thereafter, I headed to Palace Iron Man. The beauty and splendour of the residential cum commercial building enthralled me, as the majestic façade and decorations spoke volumes about the rich history. Content about spending an adventurous day, though I was dead on my feet, there was a smile on my face as I returned to my hotel room.

Time is a fickle thing. When you are at peace and enjoying yourself, time seems to have wings. But when you are facing the toughest times, it seems to be a tortoise. And that was exactly the case with me. It seemed to move fast when I was creating the most wonderful memories in my life. The visit was etched in my memory and the experience was rejuvenating; so much so that I planned to visit the neighbouring cities during my next vacation. Soon, I packed my bags for my return flight to Kyiv, even though I was exhausted. However, I had no option as I had to get my mandatory COVID test twenty-four hours prior to the journey. So, I freshened up and left for the airport.

While I was reminiscing about the wonderful times of the trip, I was in for a rude shock; the test results came back positive. I sat lonely on a wooden bench, on the beautiful path in front of the hospital, wondering what to do. I had to act immediately or miss my flight. So, I dialled up a few known contacts and asked for their suggestions. Each one advised me to stay back in quarantine.

Once I realised that I could do nothing about the situation and the flight would be missed anyway, I booked a room in another hotel. I had to stay back in Belgrade, locked up in my room again, in a different land, with no one around to care for me or no known faces to make me feel at home. All the euphoria of my short trip flew out of the window, and a sense of dread of the unknown filled me.

Desolation seeped in as I informed my parents, who fretted about it. Though I was also a bit shaken, I assured them that there was nothing to worry about. With the promise to keep them posted, I got mentally prepared to lock myself up in the hotel room for the next ten days. Dire situations are life's way of reminding you to pause and ascertain the path you want to tread on.

Popping in a few tablets, I rested for the day, hoping to get well soon. As I said, life was throwing surprises at me for which I was unprepared. I was in my hotel room taking regular medicines and resting. Despite that, I did run a temperature and had cough. This terrified me as I didn't know what to do if my health deteriorated. Thankfully, it was only for a day, and though I did feel a bit sluggish, there were no other significant symptoms.

The time was crawling at a snail's speed. All that I could do was spend my time reading books, watching the news, movies, and listening to songs. Still, after a few days, when the situation got on my nerves and I was bored and feeling miserable, I ordered a sumptuous cake and treated myself. The cake was from a famous bakery in Belgrade, Hleb & Kifle. The taste still lingers in my mouth when I think of Belgrade. Food is therapeutic and has the power to uplift one's spirits even in the most trying times. The moment I took a bite, I was transported back to the time when I came across this place for the first time.

I had been passing by the shop. That is when I saw a lot of people waiting. Intrigued, I stood aside for some time and then realised they were all waiting for their turn to taste the cakes. The huge crowd was proof enough that the taste must be mouthwatering. I, too, was tempted and thought of trying out a small piece of Belgian chocolate and waited in the queue. Though it took a while before my turn came, it was worth the wait. The first bite of the chocolate made me feel like heaven on earth; it was so delicious and tempting that my taste buds exploded with flavour. It was the best Belgian chocolate I had in my life so far. I couldn't resist and took a picture of my first bite. When I had shared it with my friends and described it, they had all been green with envy. It was that first bite which tempted me to order a whole cake when I felt depressed during quarantine.

Days seemed to stretch longer and painfully slower than they appeared. However, in that state, I didn't forget to count my small blessings, as, except for that one day when I had a temperature and a bit of cough, I was fine otherwise. I took another test on the ninth day, praying for the tests to be negative. Everyone prays to pass a test, but this was the first time in my life I prayed to fail. I'm sure most of the people would've done the same during COVID. Thankfully, the results came out to be negative. My joy knew no bounds, as, at last, the ordeal was over. Within no time, I booked my return flight to Kyiv so that I could fly on the very next day and informed my parents about it as well.

I was counting the minutes when I would again be in Kyiv, my second home, and desperately prayed that life would offer me no more surprises.

CHAPTER – 3

"Set peace of mind as your highest goal, and organise your life around it."

— Tao-Porchon-Lynch

Kyiv, my home, was calm and peaceful with a mild haze hovering above the city line. I landed in the city in the morning on 22 February. The chirping of birds, as they went about with their routine, was a harmony to my ears. I reached my home and slumped on the chair. Tiny streaks of sun rays crept inside the shielded glass, piercing their way through the clouded sky. A peaceful smile adorned my face as I gazed outside the window at the beautiful city that changed my life. The calmness and beauty this place embraced were reflected in the hearts of the people.

Though I missed the noisy clutter that is an ingrained part of India — the noisy chit-chats of nosy aunties, the banter of the loud uncle gangs, the bickering of the naughty kids, the never-ending bargaining of the home-makers, and the constant honking of the wheels — I loved the peace Kyiv showered me with. The place was serene and refreshing to the soul. It wasn't a piece of cake to live alone in a new city, without knowing its language and culture. I had my own set of challenges to face and hurdles to cross. Yet, all I can say when I think of Kyiv is 'beautiful'.

Today, when I think back to my university days, I realise how much Ukraine has moulded me into the better person I am now. Life is the best teacher. It tends to throw all the chaos your way; it is up to you to drown in grief or stay afloat and make it to the other side.

Splashing cold water on my face, I filled up a hot cup of coffee and sat by the window, watching the city come to life. As I reclined back on my chair, I recollected the day, around six months back, when I stood in front of my Dean, reliving the feeling of how it felt to be known as Nitin Chopra and not *Tolka* Nitin. The memory came alive in front of my eyes as I could still remember every small detail.

***

That day, I had flung open the door, feet

tapping hard against the smooth marble floor and my heart thudding in joy. After years of endless struggle and hurdles, a simple yet valued piece of paper, worth deciding my future, was going to be in my hands. As I stepped in, my glance fluttered to the signboard, carrying the bold carved letters 'Dean's Office'.

When I greeted her, she looked at me with a warm smile, her doe-shaped eyes peeking above her perfectly-rimmed glasses. Keeping aside her thick pile of papers, she focused her attention on me. I then stated the purpose of my visit. She pulled one file from the huge stack of files and skimmed through the inked words, her eyes stopping at a certain point. She looked back at me with a hint of uncertainty and then back at the file, seemingly pondering over something for a while.

"Tolka Nitin?!" her melodic voice posed a question laced with amusement.

I nodded. She was astonished and exclaimed, "Quite interesting. I usually hear very long Indian names that are difficult to pronounce. But *Tolka* Nitin! Interesting."

She cross-checked the contents and asked me to wait outside for a while, till she got the documents ready. My feet skipped in joy, and every step of mine was filled with excitement as I thanked her and walked out on that day, awaiting to receive my degree.

****

Life is never full of roses. It comes with thorns too. Never for a minute had I thought how the city's future, including mine, would be turned upside down, in the next second of the clock. When I thought the toughest storms of my life had passed, and finally, I had settled well, life proved me wrong. Alas! Little did I know that it was the calm before the storm.

Then again, 'storm' didn't justify what lay ahead. It was a tornado, destroying the entire country, trampling over the dreams and lives of innumerable people along with it. War not only takes lives but also the hope, positivity, and innocence of the survivors.

CHAPTER – 4

"All forms of violence, especially war, are totally unacceptable as means to settle disputes between and among nations, groups, and persons."

— Dalai Lama XIV

22 February 2022, a day before our lives were turned upside down. I was on my way back from the Indian embassy accompanied by my legal advisor. He was the one who had helped me with the proceedings from the start of my medical career. We were returning after taking care of the administrative paperwork. For the last few days, even during the trip, I had heard titbits of news about the strong possibility of a Russian invasion of Ukraine but didn't pay heed. But now, the news was spreading like wildfire. That made me quiver in my boots, as God forbid, if it happened, there might soon be a war situation.

I was fervently hoping and praying that things would go smoothly so that the war would never happen. While discussing the same with him, I noticed that his face was dull. He heaved a sigh and murmured, "It's coming, and I'm sure about it. Not in the distant future, but now, when you least expect it."

The discussion was disturbing. Even after I reached home, his words kept reverberating in my mind. No war can ever be justified. No matter who wins, the negative aspects far outweigh the positive ones. As a precautionary measure, I decided to buy some groceries and the necessities in case something unexpected happened. Unable to sit quietly at home, I took my dog, Penny, and went out for a walk to the nearby park. Though it had been only a month since I adopted her from my friend, I had become quite fond of her. The evening breeze was so cool and calm that it had the ability to pacify anyone.

I was composed and even laughing at my dog's cute little stunts but had an unsettling feeling inside me. The tranquillity in the surrounding was priceless. I looked around the park, as the ominous words rang in my head. *It's coming, and I am sure about it.* My heart and mind were in constant discord with each other. I couldn't help but gaze around, trying to imprint the joyous moments of this place in my mind. I soaked up as much as my eyes could and once again prayed that nothing would happen. Most times, our sixth sense is way more powerful than credited. Rather, the voice is ignored or shushed for one's own peace of mind.

The place was filled with people, a few jogging around while a few were walking leisurely. A couple of families were randomly seated on the grass with their kids, laughing and playing with not a care in the world. The kids' faces shone brightly, reflecting their innocence like a mirror. Two other kids were playing with a ball when my dog accidentally ran into them, causing one of them to fall. Though his knee got bruised, without shedding a tear or throwing tantrums, he happily got up, dusted his knee, and smiled. When I apologised, he waved at me and ran away. His parents too gave a warm smile without causing a ruckus.

For a minute, I thought a huge drama would be played out by the kids' parents, and I'd be the centre of attraction of the whole city. Thankfully, no such untoward incident happened with me. I'd witnessed some instances where the mother had been flapping her hands in the air, cursing the person who caused the damage. It'd even extend to a situation where she'd beat her hands against her chest and forehead and then drum them back on the ground. So, no, I was not imagining things. I understood that people express love differently. The language of love is unique and differs from person to person, and I'd learnt this one from many of my experiences.

Thinking about how peace-loving and outgoing these people were, I moved further into the park. I saw a few couples, both the elderly ones who were sitting on the benches holding each other lovingly, as well as the young ones, who were blushing and whispering into each other's ears.

I sat in a silent unoccupied place in front of the lake. Penny immediately jumped on my lap and signalled me to pet him. Rubbing his head and looking at the calm waters, I was lost in thoughts of how hard it had been to convince my family to allow me to study abroad.

***

In 2015, my parents had been busy hunting for a well-recognised university to push me in, like most school graduates' parents. I had successfully taken a step ahead in my life and was now out in the world, ready to face life's challenges. Freshly passed out of school with flying colours, I was eager to step into the next phase of my life. Meanwhile, my parents, like any typical *desi* ones, bustled around to enrol me in a reputed Medical University. I, on the other hand, wished to step out of the cocoon and explore and conquer the land beyond the borders. It wasn't an easy nut to crack, but I did. Finally, after a huge round of deliberation that went on for months, I convinced my family to let me study abroad. The peace in my heart and soul proved that I had made the right decision.

Having no other option, my parents sat with me, surfing the net to get hold of a good university. After what felt like ages, we got in contact with a person who helped us with all the registrations and admissions. Since it was uncharted territory, I was excited and nervous at the same time. I was praying for everything to proceed well without any hurdles.

Before we realised it, a month flew by. I received my visa acceptance, so the next step was getting the flight tickets. Air Astana's tickets were booked for a 10 am flight on 8 September 2015. We packed my stuff and arranged it in order, while my mom kept dropping fresh tears. However, my dad stood brave. Although worried sick, he didn't exhibit his feelings. Thereafter, we visited our village and bid farewell to all my relatives and friends.

It was on the last night that I felt the jitters. Throughout the night, I kept tossing and turning on my bed. My head kept popping with memories of the time I spent growing up here in Panipat. The nervousness of stepping foot into a new country, where a new culture prevailed, left me sleepless. The language of the country was yet to be learned by me. Also, the people were bound to have different dispositions as compared to India. The anxiety and pressure I felt that night were too much to handle. Settling away from home can be an unsettling feeling. But if one wants his name to be heard by the world, there is no option but to step out of his comfort zone. Leaving everything to God and hoping everything would turn out in my favour, I let my dreary eyes shut and catch up on sleep for a few hours.

On the way back home, my uncle and aunt joined us to see me off at the airport. One of my dad's closest family friends, Amit Shah Dilbagi, called up and not only showered his love but also put in a few words of the most needed advice. Those words are still etched in my mind. 'Never disrespect your parents. You may be at a faraway place more advanced than where they grew up. But that doesn't mean you know what they do. If you can't share something with your parents, then know that is wrong. Care for your parents even when you are busy.'

For me, my parents will always be on the highest pedestal, as no matter what, they raised me with all they had and went beyond their means to provide me with the best.

I glanced at my home one last time and tried to etch the memory deep in my heart. I got in the car, and like a convoy of high-profile politicians, we drove through the roads of Panipat.

I looked out of the window at the familiar path and the trees that seemed to wave goodbye to me. My heart felt heavy to leave behind the place I loved the most. I was trying hard to control the tears that made their way to my eyes. Lost in my thoughts, I didn't realise that the car had arrived at the airport.

Giving a tight hug to my mom and dad, savouring their proximity, I said my farewells with tears pooling in my eyes. Before checking in, I hugged my dad one more time and told him, "Dad, you have done a lot for me so far. Now, it's my time to look after myself. I'll try my best to take care of all the things. Don't worry."

With a proud smile, he let me walk inside the well-polished glass doors of the airport.

Going past the security guards and after getting my identity checked, I entered and stood in the long queue to get my bags weighed before getting my boarding pass. Through the glass doors, we kept glancing at each other every now and then. We stayed on call, and my parents were listening to everything happening inside. I, too, was listening to all they were talking about. When I put my luggage on the machine, it showed that the weight was a wee bit more than what was permissible.

Thinking of a solution, I quickly opened my bag and took out the bulky leather jacket, wearing it above my formal attire. The luggage's weight decreased while mine increased by 1.5 kgs. Over the call, I heard my father's friend, Krishan uncle, say to my dad, "Magic happens when one enters through these gates. You become smart and bring the best out of yourself when you choose to go to a foreign land on your own. Put your worries aside. He will handle everything hereafter."

Maybe these situations are common, but for parents, it is a proud moment when they see their kids solving problems on their own. His words still echoed in my ears, and I wonder if I was smart enough to be complimented.

***

The chirping of a bird as it flew back home, pulled me out of my reverie. For a while, I had been transported back to the phase after which my life changed forever.

As it was getting dark, I had a hearty meal and then retired to the comfort of my home, unaware of the approaching disaster. I went into a deep slumber, hugging the comforter, not knowing that I'd be craving such a night of blissful sleep in the forthcoming days.

CHAPTER – 5

"The real and lasting victories are those of peace and not of war."

— *Ralph Waldo Emerson*

 My head was tilted against the wall, my eyes still shut, as I reminisced about the days right before disaster struck. Flashes of the scary dream which woke me up yesterday morning, managed to jolt me once again, and I opened my eyes as shivers ran down my spine. Maybe the nightmare was a manifestation of my collective thoughts that revolved around the conversation I had with my legal advisor the other day, or maybe it was my fear and insecurity, or a premonition; I couldn't figure out.

It was now that I could relate why I saw the park in the nightmare; the apprehension of losing the tranquillity that prevailed in the city caught up and reflected in the terrible dream. I gazed around at the strained faces and knew that the ominous dream was no longer just a dream. Though the situation hadn't reached the stage of destruction, if matters got out of hand, it wouldn't take long for that to happen.

Minutes passed and turned into hours, and hours into night. I shuddered as I thought of what would have happened if subway stations and other public gathering places would have been targeted. If they would have been bombarded, we all would have lost our lives in a fraction of a second, clueless and unaware as to what transpired.

Luckily, the three bombs that targeted Kyiv fell on unoccupied buildings, airport runways, military infrastructure, and other unpopulated areas. The properties and the parked vehicles were heavily damaged. The roads were cracked and fire erupted from the damaged electrical wirings and gas pipelines. However, no lives were lost, and we were thankful for that. Fortunately, as night neared, the alarms went off, and we were ushered out of the subway and back to our homes.

I thought that the threat was contained and was relieved for a fleeting moment until I switched on the net. Messages flooded from my friends in Kharkiv and the ones who were staying near the borders. While we were safe in the shelter, the citizens living near the borders and the soldiers guarding those areas had lost their lives.

I grieved for the bereaved families. The soldiers, who didn't bother about their lives to protect their countrymen, had to pay the penalty. However, the bullets that pierced through the soldiers not only hit them but their entire family too.

Initially, there were only messages from friends and fellow residents. But soon, there was a flood of national and international media reporters, releasing news articles along with pictures and videos of the destruction.

Resting my head on the pillow, I couldn't help but release my pain in the form of tears as I felt contempt for people for whom victory is the only motive in life. But in my opinion, cowards choose war as the first step!

Trying to get over the negativity that was threatening to drown me, I reminisced about how joyous I had felt when I had first landed in Kyiv.

***

It had been around midnight by the time my flight landed. Along with my friends, I waited near the conveyor belt to pick up my luggage. A smile erupted on my face when the others were trying to locate their luggage while I could spot mine even from a considerable distance. All thanks to my dad, who made it easy to identify them, as he had marked my name on the bag in huge letters with a bright-coloured marker.

Within no time, the luggage was collected and we moved towards the exit. A gust of cool breeze welcomed us as we stepped outside the airport. The chilling weather was quite contrasting to the blazing hot winds of India. The jacket I had worn proved to be a saviour as it kept me warm and comfortable while my friends were shivering. The feeling of looking like a joker was replaced by being intelligent as I stood grinning at my friends.

Though tired due to the long flight, the excitement of a new life in a different nation kept me wide awake. I was looking forward to the new phase of life, creating memories, and establishing acquaintances in Kyiv. I had dared to step out of my realm, ready to take on the world with renewed vigour, hoping to achieve the great dreams I had seen for myself.

All the students who had arrived from India, were gathered at one place, and from there, they took us to our university on a separate bus. My eyes glimmered with joy while my heart was filled with unexplainable emotions. Though it was midnight and the scenic beauty was moderately visible, the city was still beautiful. Lights from the shut office buildings and the moving vehicles, traffic lights and street lights guiding the commuters, and night lamps glowing in front of the sleeping residents twinkled like the stars in the night sky.

The roads were smooth and clean. The litter was neatly collected in an organised manner at the allotted spots. Vehicles were being manoeuvred smoothly, passing through the traffic lights. Unlike the restless honking vehicles and the impatient drivers in the traffic jams that I was used to seeing, there were no jams here. Traffic rules were being followed perfectly. The drivers had patience, and the horns were honked only when needed. I fell in love with this place at first sight and was eagerly looking forward to the upcoming years of my medical journey.

My bus ride came to an end, and we were moved into a huge main hall for instructions. For our meal, we were provided rice, bread, and buttermilk to satiate our thirst and hunger. Alas! It wasn't as good as expected. Like every other hostel food, this too was bland and tasteless. It was then that our taste buds realised the value of home-cooked meals. Nonetheless, we had to eat whatever we were provided with. That moment made me wonder if we had come from riches to rags in a day. I missed my mom so much and was feeling quite depressed.

I shut my eyes for a moment and pictured my mom standing in the kitchen, toiling for hours to make the delicious food that I was missing so badly right now.

At that point, I didn't know how I would survive on such unpalatable food for the next five years.

Later, after the formal instructions, we were sent to our respective hostel rooms. The hostel was not up to my expectations, crushing my hopes that things would be different here. Be it the food or the room, nothing was like home. We think places other than home would be joyful and exciting, but only when we step outside of our comfortable home, we realise that it is the best place and that's why it's called 'home'.

We silently settled down and had to retire to bed. This tiny bit of bitterness made me a tad bit worried and made me doubt myself whether I had made the right decision by insisting to come here. I had the urge to immediately rush back to India and spend the days in my comfort zone. But there was no way out now. I had no option but to lead my life here, since a huge amount of money was spent on my education and travel to Kyiv. Also, the pride in my parents' eyes that I had the guts to choose this path, made me refrain from thinking along those lines. Somehow, digesting the hard facts, I informed my family about my safe arrival and went to sleep.

***

It is indeed true that one understands the value of a person or a place in its absence.

Reminiscing the olden days was brought to a sudden halt when my mobile rang, and the caller ID displayed the name of my friend from Kharkiv. He was not the one who would call unnecessarily. Looking at the time, my gut twisted in knots, afraid something had happened to him.

CHAPTER - 6

"If we don't end war, war will end us."

— *H G Wells*

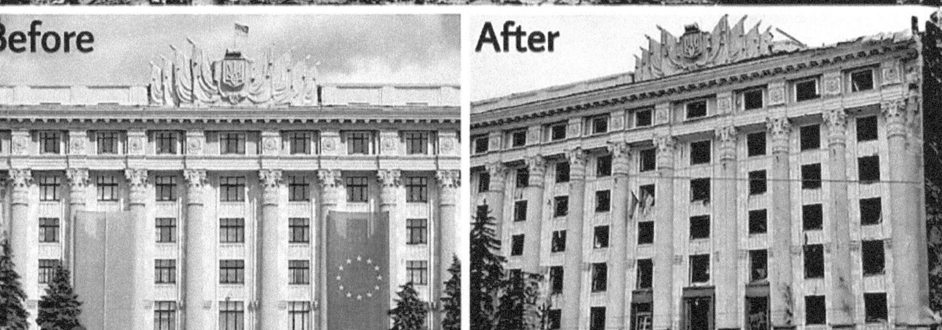

As soon as I picked up the call, I got to know that my friend in Kharkiv had become the witness of the first live bombardment in Ukraine. Though his voice didn't seem to be clogged with tears, the sadness and fright he was going through were unmistakable in the tremors in his voice as he related the gut-wrenching scenario. He was devastated, and before he could continue further, I heard the sirens from his end. He cut the call as he had to rush to a safety bunker. His call had made me anxious.

I was scrolling through the social media for some updates, when I saw that my friend had posted a few. I quickly opened his social media profiles and read the posts and stories he had posted. As if the terror in his voice was not horrifying enough, his Instagram stories and posts were proof of the barbarous acts that were being carried out.

"As usual, I woke up at three in the morning for the final exam preparation. I had put a cup of black coffee to boil. The aroma of caffeine was already helping to dissipate my sleep and providing me with the extra energy I needed. In the interim, I became aware of some weird stuff that had started to dismantle, though it took me some time to figure out what was happening. Soon, I started receiving one shock after another. The first one was a massive power outage, and the other was that Kharkiv airport was being shut down and the staff evacuated around four in the morning. Not having a clear consensus of what was happening, I decided to explore Twitter, only to find out that orders for a full-scale invasion of Ukraine had been issued." Another post read,

"I was feeling lost and out of bounds. To calm down my nerves, I took the first sip of coffee at around five in the morning. As it touched my lips, Kharkiv experienced its first major shelling. Unable to sustain my uneasiness, I opened the window. To my horror, the sky was tainted with an orange hue due to the flames rising in the air because of the continuous bombardment. I thought I was hallucinating, or maybe it was just a bad dream, and I would soon wake up from it. But much to my despair, my beloved city, Kharkiv, and I were the victims of inhumane Russian aggression. Whatever was happening was hard to believe, and all I could think was that this was a phase. I stayed back in my apartment, thinking it might stop and wouldn't continue for long. However, I was only trying to deceive myself. It wasn't the end; it was just the beginning. The beginning of another massive era of terror and fright."

His revelations shook me to the core. Still, I somehow composed myself and texted him to find a way to get to safety before the situation went out of hand.

While the children of the rest of the world were reading the history of World War I and II, the children of Ukraine were being made the victims of their next history lessons. Petrified by the enormity of all that was going on, I switched to the other websites and scrolled through the headlines and videos. Several headlines flashed in big bold letters.

'Putin announces to start military operations against Ukraine'

"The invasion has begun," Ukraine's Interior Ministry confirmed. On the other hand, Putin said that he seeks 'demilitarisation' of Ukraine but has no plans to occupy it.

- The New York Time

One after the other, I kept reading the headlines by the leading media houses.

"The invasion of Ukraine has effectively already begun," Morrison said. "Russia is at peak readiness to now complete a full-scale invasion of Ukraine, and that is likely to occur within the next 24 hours.

- CN

"His ultimate goal is to destroy Ukraine. He's not interested in parts of Ukraine. He is not interested in even keeping the entire country under his control," Kubela said during a live interview with CNN's Jake Tapper.

- CN

This made me think that some leaders seek glory in war, in death, in destruction, only because they themselves remain untouchable by those destructions.

With shivering fingers, I swiped the dreadful pictures that were shared along with the news. It took me immense courage to see them. They were not unlike the several war pictures that are available all over the net, but for me, they were devastating. They had hit home, and I was not able to accept it. This involved the places I had walked on, had fun, and created wonderful memories for a lifetime.

They were the once peaceful and breathtaking places I lived in. but now, bodies of dead people were lying on the streets, while blood was oozing out, forming a pool around their heads. The legs of a few were bent and dislocated in weird angles, whereas the bones of a few bodies stuck out, whose lower halves were mutilated.

Soldiers lay on the ground, blood gushing out through the several bullet-pierced holes. A few others had heavy metal rods and demolished building walls resting on their motionless bodies, too heavy for their fragile bodies to bear.

Cyclists and bikers lay on the ground with bullets in their heads, the lower half seated on the cycle whereas the upper half was lying on the ground. While all this was shattering, there were a few pictures that made my blood boil. I was utterly shocked thinking about the cruel nature of mankind. I had heard and read of the torments a soldier had to go through if caught by the enemy nation; even for a trained soldier, it would have been torturous. Imagine how it would be for a civilian to go through the same!

The videos which my friend had shot added fuel to the fire. Before I could get up and gather my strength for the next catastrophe, life sneaked up on me, as it meted out blow after blow, without giving even a minute to gain some semblance. The Russian forces were swiftly moving into the civilisation areas after destroying the military targets.

Missiles rained down on the residential apartments, turning the huge buildings to dust and ashes in the blink of an eye. Armed men were seen roaming the streets while the tanks progressed into the capital. Residents were imprisoned inside their homes, as they were too afraid to go out. Home — a place that is supposed to be safe, was no longer a haven for most. Fear of death paralysed the once merry Ukrainians.

On the first day, the place which provided shelter to me, turned out to be a nightmare for the others, terrorising them for the rest of their lives. Heaps and heaps of shattered glasses lay on the road. Fiery reddish-orange flames were burning bright from the rubble of wrecked buildings. The vehicles parked outside were burning as they had been fuelled by the missiles. Bullets from gunshots marked their imprint on the car doors, whereas the roads were cracked. The once green and blooming trees were now lifeless and leafless, scorched from the heat, not of the sun, but from the blazing heat of the insatiable hunger of the power to control.

I slumped down, closing my eyes for a while, unable to take it anymore. The most tragic part is that a soul once broken continues to walk this earth, a hollow vessel of its former self. It bears this invisible weight, this unbearable pain, and keeps it hidden from the world, locked away in the depths of its heart.

CHAPTER – 7

"All I have is memories, and all that they do is haunt me."

— *Sumaya Enyegue*

I was on my way to the university. It was taking me longer than usual. When I took a turn at the far end of the road, the weather seemed to become monstrous. Dark grey clouds clumped together at lightning speed, making the day appear as if it was night. I ran faster to avoid the sinister darkness looming over my head. Dread washed over me at the sight of people lying everywhere on the streets. Dead. I was too scared and shocked to run further and turned back to return on the same path I came from, but I was lost. I came to a dead-end. It was as if life was telling me, 'It's not worth going back to the past. Life has to move forward, even if it seems uncertain.'

Not knowing what to do, I took another turn and ran frantically, where I saw kids crying beside the dead bodies. This road too seemed to come to an end but the sight of bushes gave me some hope. Just when I thought there would be no path to move forward, I saw a forest beyond the end of the road. I had no option but to cross the bushes and enter the forest. As I entered, I caught a glimpse of the Karpathian mountains in Ukraine. I had visited this mountain once during my university days. It seemed to be pulling me towards it.

Back then, when I had reached Hoverla, the highest peak in Ukraine, I felt a sense of tranquillity wash over me and indulged myself in a few minutes of meditation. I sought to seek peace within and not get pulled into the storm whirling around me. My mind was filled with complete calmness and peace after I meditated there. I felt the same peace consume me when I had entered the forest and caught a glimpse of the mountain. But it was only for a fleeting moment.

The next moment, I saw myself waiting in the queue to worship the idols in Mehndipur Balaji temple in India. What seemed to be odd was, I was in the line, waiting for many hours but at the same spot. The line seemed to have stuck at the same place. While waiting, I observed the surrounding areas, taking in the sight of the temple walls, the idols' placement, the boundaries, and the entrances into each idol's chamber.

***

I was still waiting in the queue when the dream came to an abrupt end and I jerked awake. It was very frustrating and baffling for me as I couldn't understand how I could dream about that particular temple, as I had never ever visited it in my life! I immediately googled up the temple's name and looked up the pictures, videos, and the history of it. What I saw online made my heart spike up its beat. The entire architecture of the temple was exactly the same as I saw in my dream, with not even a minute change.

To my astonishment, I knew every entrance into the idol chamber, every turn to take and where it led, every idol placed inside the temple premises, and even the waiting area where people had to stand in the queue. It was the exact replica of my dream. I kept looking wide-eyed at the screen, unable to understand what the dream meant or how it was possible to know the temple even though I had never visited in real life. Life has its own ways to reassure our faith and hope. I tried to pay heed to the dream; guess this was life's way of intensifying my faith in the Almighty.

I was still lost in my thoughts when the sirens started blaring again. My mind was blank for a moment, unable to grapple with what was happening. Bright flashes of blue and red light reflected through my window pane, the ringing of alarms and sirens getting louder and louder with each passing minute. The sound of the underground bunkers of my building being opened and the fast and loud footsteps of rushing people echoed through the empty stairways. I was petrified and immobilised, not knowing what to do next.

Luckily, I was saved by a knock on my door. My neighbour was kind enough to check on me amidst this rising chaos. He was an elderly gentleman, around my father's age. Generally, he was a cheerful man with two sons and four grandkids. Two of them were well-settled in the US. Unfortunately, his elder son and his granddaughter had chosen this month to visit him. The usual warmth in his eyes was missing, and the crinkled pyjamas mirrored the wrinkles on his forehead. Uncertainty and the urge to keep his family safe were distinct in his eyes. I was able to feel the agony he was going through. During all this time, his smiling face seemed to be a stranger to grief and apprehension, but this one incident was enough to have shaken him up. Not only he but also, people, who had believed no one can harm the innocent, were questioning their beliefs now.

He advised me to carry blankets, some warm clothes and food to eat, besides my mobile phone and chargers, in case the stay in the bunker took longer than expected. I quickly gathered the things and rushed with him to the bunker.

It is in moments like these, the true self of people is reflected. I was grateful to that man who considered others' safety too. This was the first time in my life I experienced what hiding for safety really meant. Bunkers that were non-functional for many years, were now open and packed with people. The air was thick, filled with terrifying noises. People in my building had brought their tiny bags packed and ready to flee when the need arises. Looking at them, I realised how unprepared I was. Though the government had advised us to carry a backpack to come in handy when the need to leave the country arises, I was under the illusion that things wouldn't go out of the hands.

I glanced around the basement in bewilderment. Couples sat cuddled together, as if cherishing their last moments. Older people sat with scrunched-up faces that revealed their inner turmoil. Babies were bundled in blankets and kids rolled up in fur coats sat hugging their parents, while a few had brought their pets too. Many were immersed in the news on their mobiles, trying to get the status of the current situation. Collective whispers and murmurs of finding a way to escape reverberated throughout the room. Their journey was one of internal storm, where emotions were deconstructed and rebuilt to lay bare the essence of their humanity.

I found a free corner and nestled up against the wall. Bringing my knees closer to my chest, I rested my head and got lost in the wonderful memories of my first year at my university.

***

The first official day on the new land turned out to be adventurous for us. We were yet to learn the language of the country, and communication was very difficult. With crisp shirts and formal pants, neatly trimmed hair and beards, my friends and I stood in front of the huge building which was supposed to change our fates. The sight of the peach-painted building shrunk my heart. How could I have been so mistaken? I had painstakingly gone through each detail.

The campus had looked so different in the pictures! Disappointment seeped in as I had flown across the seas to experience a new taste of life. But I was upset. Gazing at the surrounding greenery, we walked further, only to be pleasantly surprised. My shrunken heart was once again full-blown with excitement and energy as we had a glimpse of the main college campus. Later, we came to know that the previous building we had seen was the administrative block.

Oh, yeah! This is what I'd call the vibe of a foreign land. It was like a diamond shielded by charcoal. Once the tour of the campus was complete, we were left to fend for ourselves. We met a few new students there at the campus who looked a lot like Indians and started conversing in Hindi. They had confused looks on their faces, and there was no reply from any of them. Only when we changed to English, we got to know that they were from Yemen, Canada, and Cuba. A little while later, we came to know that Ahmed Al Kuhali, Khaled Lutf, Kennedy, and Mario Menchero Robles were in our group. We laughed at our stupidity. After receiving the schedules for the upcoming days, we left.

Since we had the first day off, we thought of sightseeing. The locality was lovely and uplifted our spirits. The daytime was as spectacular as the night view had promised. We were like kids excited to see the outside world, unperturbed by the fact that we couldn't communicate at all. We had to use hand signs to buy things and to travel.

Like a bird let loose out from its cage, we were exploring the beautiful city, unaware that a few years later, we would be craving serenity. Roaming around the Main Independence Square, Maidan Nezalezhnosti, situated at the Kyiv city centre, we glanced at the endless shops, showcasing a wide variety of merchandise. Though it was the main hub area, it wasn't as crowded as the market streets of India.

While we were near the railway station, one of my friends, Rishabh, got to know that his phone was missing. When he was boarding the bus, someone flicked his phone out of his pocket and ran away. By the time he realised it, the bus had almost started and the thief was already far ahead. Since the bus was crowded and the thief was out of reach by then, he accepted that it would be difficult for him to run behind the thief to catch him. The newly launched iPhone, which he had recently bought, was thankfully at his home in India. Hence, instead of following the thief, he let him go.

By afternoon, we were walking back to our hostel when we noticed a girl dressed in ripped skinny jeans, a figure-hugging sleeveless t-shirt, and high heels, walking towards us. She had a sly smile on her face and an innocent look in her eyes. She was so close to us, we could smell her sweet perfume. While we kept ogling at her, she walked by us.

My friend, Rishabh, felt a touch on his back pocket. Probably because of the disaster earlier in the day, his reflexes were quick enough to catch the girl's hand. But the girl was swifter than us. She had pick-pocketed my friend's purse and hurriedly passed it on to her accomplice, who fled from there in the blink of an eye.

As we confronted her, she started screaming and accusing us of trying to harass her. A few passers-by were shooting weird and disgusting glances at us, while a few others didn't bother about what was going on. We were lucky that a crowd hadn't gathered, accusing us, as we wouldn't have been able to even defend ourselves! The girl kept shouting and blaming us in her native language. Though we understood there were a few curse words in each sentence, it had no effect on us, as we were not at fault. It was like watching an animated movie.

If we would have continued arguing, we would have landed up at a police station on the very first day. We were already tired enough. Being clueless as to how to get ourselves out of this situation, my friend let her leave without creating a scene. However, he immediately called up the bank back in India and blocked all the credit cards he had in his stolen wallet.

After a while, when we came back to the hostel, the guard stopped us to inform that someone had left Rishabh's wallet with him. My friend took the wallet from the guard and checked all the contents. He noticed that his cards and all the other stuff were there except the money. The fact that he got his wallet back astounded all three of us, and we stared at each other. The next moment, we broke out into a loud fit of laughter. It was scary, and at the same time, this adrenaline rush was an exciting experience.

"Oh, man! How did you get so lucky to get robbed twice on the same day?!' I exclaimed, and a new round of laughter echoed in our room. It was a peculiar start to making memories that I would cherish for a lifetime.

***

A loud yell pulled me out of my reverie. It wasn't a terrified one; rather, a happy yell. The sirens had finally stopped, and we felt relieved. Thanking God, we went back to our apartments, hoping that the situation wouldn't arise again. Scared of the unforeseen future, we hoped this would come to an end soon. However, the circumstances were gloomy and unpredictable, and we didn't know for sure whether we will be taking our next breath or not.

CHAPTER - 8

"And darkness and decay and the red death held illimitable dominion over all."

—Edgar Allan Poe

The days were like a second round of quarantine, locked inside our rooms. Both times, lives were at stake, but this time, there was no cure; it was either flee or die. None knew how it would end or how long the destruction would continue. Hiding in the safety bunkers didn't assure us of our survival. The fear of a bomb dropping near us persisted all the time in our hearts, scaring the daylights out of us. Whenever I peeped out of the window, I would be greeted with deserted streets. Yet, from afar, I could catch a glimpse of the jammed roads lined up with vehicles. The blaze of the sun's rays was not as bright as the flames that changed the hue of the sky.

The days when the whole world was in panic were crystal clear in my mind. The news was flooding with multiple things at the same time — uncountable deaths, several people being hospitalised, innumerable frantic calls in search of medicines and hospital beds — all in a fraction of a second. Huge amounts of money were being exchanged. While the affluent families managed to evade the crisis, the mediocre and the poor ones couldn't. The pain of being lonely in this horrendous world where humanity had died a silent death was more gut-wrenching than could be imagined.

With no contact with the outside world, people were losing their sanity. But the present crisis was the least bit similar to the COVID situation, because it was humanity which had gone for a toss here. Even the richest couldn't escape the fired bullets. The times had changed enormously. The time when people craved to be with a fellow human was swapped to the time when people feared the other. While the entire world witnessed the highest level of atrocities, we lived through them.

The eyes of the people were hollow, devoid of all the dreams they had ever seen. The desire to be safe and lead a peaceful life with the family within the four walls of the home was replaced by the determination to save at least one in the family. Parents had shipped their kids with other families who managed to cross the borders. The knowledge that their kids were safe was more than enough for them to accept a peaceful death. Death, suicide, or sacrifice? I wondered what would be the correct word for all the lost lives. Perhaps, murder would suit the best.

News of the Russian troops reaching Kyiv blasted from the speakers of my TV. They were near the Obolon and Heroiv Dnipra subway, which were merely a few metres away from my previous apartment. Russian tanks were parked in the surrounding areas. Tanks with huge machine guns — the ones I had seen only in movies and Republic Day parades — were moving ahead to reach the other target areas. Those paraded war tanks had seemed so peaceful and cinematic to watch, somehow assuring us that we were safe in case something happened. I had never dreamed of having to face one or imagined that they would look this terrifying. It wouldn't take long for them to come to where I was staying now. Images of my nightmare flashed across my eyes; blood dripping from the walls, bodies lying everywhere, wrapped in white cloth.

My body trembled at the thoughts of bloodshed and the stench of carcasses. But what was even more unnerving was the trauma that those who are left behind have to face. Wars get over, the dead stay dead, and history keeps getting repeated. It's only families and survivors who are left behind, who suffer the consequences, trauma, and nightmares. It's a perilous journey, for survivors are fragile beings who experience heartbreak unlike the rest of the world. While the world may see war and refugees as another news in their mundane life, for a war victim, it's an excruciating tear that rends their very essence. A part of their heart becomes a barren wasteland, forever untouched by the warmth of love.

My breath became rapid. Soon, my chest seemed laden with stones, and I was finding it difficult to breathe. I clutched at the nearby table for support and took in deep breaths, trying to intake as much oxygen as I could. All that I knew was, I had to leave immediately. My nightmares had already come half-true. If I failed to escape right now, I was afraid the rest would come true soon. I was having a panic attack, and though

I wished to run at full throttle, my legs were glued to the place I was standing. My vision blurred and my mind was jumbled with clashing thoughts and images. In that terrible moment, the soft tunes of the piano provided me with the much-needed courage and strength. It resurrected my dwindling hope to pull through this catastrophe. It gave me a purpose in life, the will to live, to protect what was dear to me.

I somehow comforted myself and hurried out of the apartment to look for ways to get out of Kyiv. The roads were completely blocked due to random and repeated bomb attacks. And the few roads that weren't blocked, were jam-packed. Vehicles that lined up hadn't moved an inch for the last six hours. If I chose to go on the road, then the means of escape wasn't possible. I didn't have enough cash with me either, and the ATMs were out of service. I walked for a long time, tracing my steps on various routes in search of ATMs or any service places where I could get some cash for my journey.

Though I thought over several possibilities, they didn't make sense. I knew I had to try my luck to reach the border by some route or the other. When I tried to take the path that would lead to the border, the sight that met me made me tremble. All my courage vanished into thin air as I stood there, frozen. I didn't have the spirit to move ahead. Trucks and cars on the road were charred and burnt down to pieces, covered in ashes as black as hate and envy could be.

Blood-painted doors and crumbled metal containers were strewn far from their own vehicles, seats popping out with burnt cushions. The numerous bullets that were fired from the guns were still etched in the metal doors, like a painful memory, making me remember what I had read about the Jallianwala Bagh massacre. A dusted teddy bear lay under the punctured tires of a car, probably abandoned in the hurry to flee.

A visual came in front of my eyes — a cute blue-eyed girl, covered with smut, clutching at her favourite teddy bear while her mother pulled her along. In a hurry, it fell from her hands, and she turned around, shedding tears for losing her most loved treasure. However, her mother was fretful to seek shelter for her child, the one who was an invaluable treasure for her. A thought popped into my mind — were they able to escape, or did they meet the same fate as the teddy?

I pumped in quick breaths as I couldn't get the thought out of my mind. Nevertheless, I couldn't afford to lose my tempo now and turned around to continue walking on my path on what seemed to be like a bridge.

For a moment, I stopped in my tracks. My heart bled tears when I realised it was the same pedestrian bridge where my friends and I had a crazy birthday party in the middle

of the night. The thought of those cherished moments brought a small smile to my face even at this time of sadness.

***

The day had started in a hurry for my roommates and me. We were late for our Latin class, and that particular teacher was infamous for not letting students inside the class if they were late even by a minute. To our luck, it was raining heavily when we left our room. We booked taxis but none were willing to drive in that heavy rain. So, we went for the only option we had. We ran and ran as fast as we could while the rain was getting heavier and denser with each passing minute. On the way, we quickly purchased two pairs of socks and rushed again. The clock ticked a minute past the class time when our running halted at the door. The teacher was already inside the class, ready to start her lessons. She was about to lash at us but looking at us fully drenched and puppy-eyed, she let us in, possibly the first exemption in the history of her teaching career.

A few of our classmates gave us weird stares while a few others started giggling. We went to the back table, water dripping from our clothes all the way, our water-filled shoes making sloppy squelching noises. Out of breath, we sat on our chairs and removed our shoes, poured a little water on the floor, and kept it near the window for drying along with our wet socks. Smiling sheepishly, we changed into the new socks we bought. However, we couldn't do anything about our wet clothes and somehow pushed through the rest of the day. It was almost mid-year by then, and we all were getting accustomed to the language and culture. We were still at the beginner level though.

Our batch was split into sub-groups. It was my birthday the next day, and I had invited a few of my friends. Dressing up well and keeping myself warm in a fluffy jacket, I went out with my friends, eager to deepen the bonds. After all, being with them only I felt the most comfortable; home away from home. We boarded the subway and were on our way to the party hall when we both had a crazy idea. Though we were a bit sceptical of trying it out in the beginning, the thrill of indulging in something crazy in public made us go for it.

He switched on his mobile and chose a peppy Bollywood song. There wasn't much of a crowd in the subway station. Since our station was the next stop, we decided to stand instead of sitting. We turned on the music to a high volume and started dancing. Our excitement kept getting higher. We moved our bodies in awkward steps and started laughing loudly. To add more craziness, we began singing the song aloud too. The passengers on the train were curiously looking at us. Some enjoyed the show and took videos too. In between the lines, we shouted that we were going to go viral in the next few minutes and continued our little show which didn't end there.

One of my friends met us at the station and was wondering why there was loud music and laughter. Knowing what had happened on the train, he too joined us in our madness. We went to the middle of the Pedestrian bridge known as the Park Bridge and continued our dancing party till midnight. Howling like wolves and laughing like maniacs, we had a fun blast that day, right from the start.

***

The cheerful memory and the joyous thrill I had was now tainted with bloodshed and dread. Little did I know that the place which had given us so much joy would one day be the reason for my grief. I would never be able to remember this bridge without associating it

with the gore and hatred, I was witnessing at that

moment. The cheerful memory would always be mixed with tears and terror. Notwithstanding the agony, I returned to my apartment.

CHAPTER – 9

"War is organised murder, and nothing else."

— *Harry Patch,*

Last surviving soldier of World War I

The news of Russia occupying Kyiv was heartbreaking. According to the reports, in the next fifteen hours or so, Kyiv would be under the complete control of Russia. I felt tears brimming in my eyes, as I couldn't bear the pain of my home being torn apart. The injustice and brutality were crossing all limits. Though I desperately wanted to bring an end to this massacre, the helplessness of being a lone powerless man crumpled my remaining hope.

Sirens kept warning us more than thrice at night. I kept going back and forth from home to the subway every time a siren was heard. People had come with their mats and food, expecting the worst.

I contacted friends and made some arrangements, as I realised that the only way out was via trains. With plans to leave as early as possible on the next day, I went to bed, taking the much-needed physical rest that would keep me moving in the days ahead. I was somehow convinced that all this would end when I wake up, and the world leaders would have come to terms to deal with the current situation.

I was proved wrong, yet again, when the huge blast happened near my university, close to Beresteska subway station. That day, I decided that I had to get out of the city by hook or by crook. Moreover, the frantic calls I was receiving from my family strengthened my decision. I convinced my family that I was safe and I'd be travelling to another city soon. The worry was evident in their tone, so I assured them of my safety even though I was feeling anything but safe.

Call after call kept ringing, and the notifications bar seemed to go crazy with loads of messages and news alerts popping. Quite a few were from my friends, staying near my university. They told me that the bombing on the bridge was done by the Ukrainian army to prevent the Russians from entering the main city. I felt as if a huge mountain had been lifted off my shoulders when the news of my university being safe reached me.

My university is my love, the place I cherish the most. It is the same feeling that we have for our school. We hate it when we are there, but once we leave, we miss it more than anything else. We also tend to thank our school for making us a better person and for giving us beautiful memories and friends.

My university too gave me a lifetime of memories. I improved many skills, and it taught me how to live life, unlike the book-hoarding heads. It gave me friends who were a part of my many first-time crazy adventures. It was also the place where I had met the treasure of my life. I also learnt to discern the types of people, make out how fake people could be, and how, within moments, they could change their behaviour. Overall, my university will always top the charts when it comes to having the most memorable moments in my life, and the mere thought of anything happening to that sacred place would have been like a death blow to my emotions.

***

It was around October end when I experienced the first snowfall in my life. One of my friends came running inside shouting, "Snow… snow… snow…" waking up the entire hostel. People who were used to it, grumbled a bit and went back to their beds. But the ones like my friends and me, who were so in awe of the snow, went out in the freezing weather and played with it. The snowfall was considerable, and the entire place looked as if it was covered with a white blanket. The ground as well as the trees were covered in sparkling white snow. The soft fluffy snow continued to fall from the sky, dancing in merriment as it swayed with the wind. My eyes grew a wee bit wider, glued to the sky and all around to witness this spectacle.

We took selfies and moved on to have a little snow-fight session. We picked up huge balls of snow and threw them at one another, even throwing a few inside each other's jackets. As though that wasn't enough, we slept on the snow, making patterns with our legs and hands. Passers-by looked at us as if we were people

who had escaped from an asylum. But that didn't deter us from immersing in the joy we were experiencing, so we blatantly ignored their contemptuous stares.

When we retired to our rooms, we laughed and called ourselves the fools of the century for acting like maniacs. Without a doubt, it was one of the most memorable moments in my life. I have experienced many memorable instances in Kyiv that make me nostalgic in a way that will have an eternal place in my mind.

In a couple of months, the winter came to an end, but the fun was unlimited. Once, when we were on our way back to our rooms, we came across many apple trees loaded with ripe apples. My eyes sparkled with mischief as wild thoughts ran amok through my mind, and when I exchanged looks with my friends, their eyes reflected the same thoughts. By this time, we were accustomed to each other's ways of thinking and insane thrilling ideas, so much so that words weren't needed to express what went on in our minds. Though we had money with us, and there were street vendors selling apples, the sweetness of forbidden and stolen fruits is heavenly.

Moreover, the apple tree was on the main street. We positioned ourselves under the tree and climbed on each other's shoulders, making a human ladder. The skinniest amongst us was at the top, and he plucked as many apples as he could. People passing by were staring at us, but instead of being scared, the thrill of getting caught fuelled even more excitement. We had plucked almost 5 kgs of apples and carried 'the loot' with us to our rooms, which became our midnight snack for almost a week. I doubt I have relished eating apples as much as I did then.

Over the time I spent in Kyiv, I didn't realise when I came out of my cocoon. Having been an introvert all my life, this was a new phase for me, where I didn't hold back. I dropped the façade and had the time of my life with my friends, indulging in crazy stuff that I hadn't comprehended getting into till then.

By the time the first year came to an end, we were tired of our hostel rooms. So, we decided to rent a private apartment and live together. The search for a safe apartment with low rent, that too in the vicinity of the university, went on for a few days. After a week of searching and talking to apartment owners, we were overjoyed to find a suitable one, unaware of the threat that was waiting for us. Within two days of finalising the apartment and paying the rent, we shifted our stuff from the hostel to our new place.

We lived there for nearly six to ten months. Everything in the apartment was going fine until that one fateful night. We used to order pizza from Domino's every week at midnight. That day, as usual, we had ordered pizza and were waiting for our delivery. We heard the doorbell and were confused as the delivery was here within a few minutes as compared to the usual time. Without giving it a second thought, we were delighted since we were all hungry.

Just as I was about to open the door, I heard multiple voices of laughter outside the door. My senses were alerted, and I knew something was wrong. I locked all the doors and windows tightly and informed my friends about it too. When we didn't open the door, those guys started banging and yelling at us to open. One of those guys mocked us, "Come on… Come on… Open the door. Domino's pizza is here…" while the others laughed.

We peeped out of the window and saw four guys standing with wooden sticks in their hands. They kept on calling out to open the door and were saying something which we didn't understand. The thought that they were aware of our midnight pizza deliveries sent chills down my spine. We didn't know if it was arranged by the landlord to frighten us since we were paying low rent or if someone else had planned something more dangerous. But we knew one thing for sure that this apartment was no longer safe for us and decided to shift soon.

We spent that sleepless night in fright while holding onto some kitchen knives and rolling pins, in case they broke into the house. The voices quietened down after a few hours and we peeped to see if they were still there or not. We couldn't see them, yet, we didn't risk coming out till the place had people moving around.

The next day, we had to go around again in search of a new apartment. This time, we found it easily and in a much lesser span of time. Within two days of finalising the apartment and paying rent, we shifted our stuff from the previous apartment to our new one. While we were on the way, we sensed someone following our taxi. From the rear-view mirror, we were able to recognise a car that had been following us for a long time. We asked the taxi driver to stop the car and informed him about the situation. Once he understood our dilemma, we asked him to help us out.

He started the car and increased the speed, and took quick turns, going past a few vehicles. He even took a different route to our destination than the planned one. We thought we had lost them but noticed that the car too had increased its speed and was still chasing us. This scared the wits out of us as we didn't know who they were and the purpose of it all. We were scared thinking of terrible things happening to us like the ones they show in the news and dramas. The chase continued, but despite our best efforts, we didn't manage to lose them.

To our luck, the taxi driver bypassed a traffic signal while they were stuck. We rushed to our apartment and quickly transferred our belongings from the cab. We thanked the driver and locked the doors behind us. Adrenaline was pumping high, and we were trembling out of fear. Once we calmed down and made sure that those pursuers had not caught up on us, we burst out laughing, as much out of relief as out of mirth.

It was these bad experiences that taught us to be more vigilant, something that good experiences failed to teach. Life is the best teacher, who teaches you to face storms and overcome them.

***

Nonetheless, that night, when we had our hearts in our mouths, was nothing compared to the terror I was going through now.

CHAPTER – 10

"All war is a symptom of man's failure as a thinking animal."

— *John Steinback*

I called up my other friend in Kharkiv to check up on him and inquire about the status there. The response I received was disturbing and heart-wrenching. It was as though wild animals were hunting for their prey. If mankind has stooped low and hunts each other for the power of control, then I wonder what the difference between humans and wildlife is. Over the years, wars have proven one thing — the human mind is more lethal than the weapon it created.

Meanwhile, in Kyiv, armed soldiers were walking to and fro, their senses on high alert to defend or attack when in need. This was the second time in my life I was seeing weapons in real life. Except for one other instance, it was in the documentaries, YouTube videos, and books that I had seen those war weapons. The first time I saw them was when my friend invited me to the army parade, he was participating in Rivne. Since it was a parade to showcase the defence weaponry, they hadn't intimidated me then. However, seeing them in real life this time made my nerves tingle in fear. The videos that my friend shared added salt to the injury, and an involuntary shiver ran down my spine.

Blades of helicopters and fighter jets cut through the silence of the clear skies. My eyes were still glued to the screen, when, within a blink of an eye, a huge thundering echoed as a missile hit a sleepy building, leaving a trail of dense grey smoke. In a moment, glass windows shattered and the building slowly crumpled down to rubble, taking down the clueless sleeping bodies. The cruel ammunition took pity on no one; everyone fell prey to the wrath of the missile, fuelled with greed and power.

Fiery flames burned brighter and rose from the ground, as the nearby buildings shook with tremors and smoke invaded the safe homes. Innocent lives were buried deep under the debris of bricks and rods. Soon, painful cries and frightened screams created chaos throughout the street. Neighbours in loose pyjamas and comfy slippers slipped out of their apartments into the streets, rushing in search of a safe shelter, terrorised about being the next target. This shook me to the core, and right at the moment, sirens started blaring in my area. Like the helpless citizens in the video, I, too, rushed out as soon as my wobbly legs would carry me.

God never sends a problem without a solution, they say. But should it be this hard? Maybe it is the survival of the fittest, as Darwin said.

"This is ridiculous. Completely unacceptable. Why can't they understand we are humans too like them? Where will we go now? This is our home!" As soon as I entered the bunker, I heard a young man yell, while he was immersed in his phone.

Following his loud outburst, people started hurriedly speaking about how inhumane the situation was. Things were getting out of hand. At the same time, praises for the President of Ukraine, Mr Zelenskyy, too were heard. He promised to be their hero, even when the world forgot to be his.

I quickly fished out my mobile and opened Twitter and other social media accounts. There was a new attack on Kherson. Hundreds and thousands of people had been injured and killed. Articles about the attacks and fatalities were circulated at lightning speed everywhere. Headlines and reporters praising the President of Ukraine were spreading on various social media platforms.

'While many leaders around the globe went live on television, presenting speeches, holding press conferences, and trying to stop the Russian aggression, the former television actor and comedian and the current President of Ukraine, Volodymyr Zelenskyy, had stepped to the frontlines personally along with the Ukrainian soldiers, defending his people and his nation

'Earlier in the evening, President Zelenskyy took charge as the Commander-in-chief, and along with the Ukrainian forces, was engaged in a fierce battle protecting his people. He had put his life on line to save the rest.'

'While the Russian military announced their targets as Ukrainian military bases, the innocent civilian infrastructure, schools, and hospitals were being shelled by them

---

A few videos showed citizens of Ukraine from the other Russian invasion-free cities starting to flee to safer regions. All flights were cancelled, and the airports were shut down from functioning as a precautionary measure. Ukraine was under attack from all three ways; via land, sky, and sea. So, the threats of Ukrainian passenger flights getting shot down were higher.

The other two options left to move out of Kyiv were by road or train. But that too seemed to be a tedious task. There were heavy traffic jams due to the number of people moving out, and at the same time, roadblocks to prevent Russian entry, which made the situation way worse. The trains were jam-packed, more so because only a handful were operational. A few desperate and panicked residents were walking all the way to a safer place with their trolley bags strolling behind them and their kids perched on them.

In various major cities around the globe, protestors had gathered in protest against Russian invasion. Even the Russian citizens were seen parading to the president's office with banners and flags of Ukraine. Huge boards with slogans like *'Stop the war'*, *'Free the nation'*, *'Spare the innocent lives'*, and so on, were held by protestors. They tried to do what they could in their own way to support us. But these people had to pay for their benevolence. The Russian government didn't take kindly to their display of support for Ukraine and the supporters were blocked and manhandled by the police. Nonetheless, the Russians supporting Ukraine proved that even though one may be incapable of stopping the brutality, not voicing out the opinion is an even bigger sin.

Panic rose in my throat. I had to move. And that had to be done at the earliest possible chance. My gut had this intuitive feeling that if I stayed here longer, there would be slim chances of getting out alive. But my heart ached for the people who were with me in this bunker. What would happen to them if they didn't get their chance? However, I noticed that many were ready to leave and they had already come with their packed bags.

Many contradicting news reports were being broadcasted and spread, making it hard for us to know the truth. Kharkiv, Mariupol, and Kherson became the major affected sites with the continuous assault of cluster bombs.

The strikes continued in the skies too. Aeroplanes were targeted and airports were attacked. The largest cargo aeroplane in the world, Mriya, which once helped to transport a lot of medical supplies to many countries during COVID and other calamities, was destroyed. It had the capacity to take loads of goods in one go. But now it lay broken in fragments, fumes of grey smoke and flames of blazing fire surrounding the body and the wings of the plane. Windows and fragments of the tail fin lay on the ground as crushed scrap metal pieces.

This made my soul shrivel. I think humanity died a silent death the day the first ammunition was made. Was there a purpose to such destruction? Who would benefit from it? What kind of people get happiness by taking innocent lives? Till recently, I thought I had seen it all — good-intentioned people as well as bad. But the devilish side of a human that the incident showed was not even a fragment of what I had ever experienced. This was barbarous.

CHAPTER – 11

"Nothing is more precious than peace. Peace is the most basic starting point for the advancement of humankind."

— Daisaku Ikeda

I had set my mind to leaving as soon as the sirens went off, and the only way was through the subway. I contacted a few of my friends on the other side, and they agreed to make arrangements for my stay. They promised to help me to the best of their abilities. The assurance was enough for me to push myself forward with renewed motivation. A few from the group said that the sirens would be stopped in some time. So, I mentally prepared myself to give it my all. I only had to pick up my bag and rush as fast as I could as soon as the sirens would go off.

Lack of food or clothing was the least of my worries at that time. My only focus was to get on the subway, come what may. After all, nothing is more invaluable than life. And the realisation hit home when we wondered each day whether we would be alive the next moment or not. A slight relief washed over with the thought of finally escaping this excruciating experience only to be gripped tighter in fear the next moment.

A sudden thought flashed across my mind. If I leave my apartment, how would *she* survive? She was smarter and knew how to protect herself from danger. Sadly, this peril was far beyond her understanding. As she was deaf, she must not have heard the loud bombs, but she must have sensed the tremors and smelled the terror that prevailed in the atmosphere. She was the calmer and quieter one, who never gave me any trouble. I doubted if taking her with me would be a possibility. But my heart was not wishing to leave her behind as well.

A war of conflict between practicality and emotions rose within me as I pondered over all possible options and weighed the pros and cons of each one of them. Meanwhile, the city seemed to have come to a halt as an eerie silence pervaded after long torturous hours of continuous sirens and announcements, other than the never-ending updates from the various social media platforms.

It is in the darkness we appreciate the light. It is in the sadness we appreciate joy. Only at this time of war, I realised the importance to appreciate the little joys of life. Small steps lead to huge success, inconsequential thoughts make up a great goal, and little desires tend to move us higher towards our dream. However, it is the little things that matter the most in our life, which are often neglected by most people. I have always been an introvert. So, seclusion or isolation was never an issue for me.

However, this deafening silence after hours of hearing the horrendous noise of war, shred me to pieces. This silence was the noise of impending terror, fright, and death, and was deadlier than the most lethal weapon, ripping the soul apart.

In the deadly silence, all that echoed were people's breaths and rapid heartbeats. It took us a moment to realise that we were free. However, no one was sure whether it was for a few minutes or longer. Then again, that little ray of hope of peace and respite from war pushed us to get going. We didn't wish to waste even the little tick of the second. Everyone started rolling up their mats and rushed out of the exit door with their kids safely tucked in their arms and the luggage quickly wheeling behind them.

The kind elderly neighbour patted my shoulders, and before leaving the bunker, told me to get to safety. I wanted to immediately catch the next means of exit from this city, but the thought of leaving her alone worried me the most. I didn't know when I would be back, or for that matter, if I ever will. I had to keep her safe. The least I could do was to make some arrangements in my room for her to be safe for the time period. Once I would manage to escape, I would think of ways to get her back.

Hence, I quickly went back to my room. Meanwhile, another fear gripped me. What if it wouldn't be a matter of merely a few days? What if I had to stay for a month or two? This triggered me. Till now, I had been carrying only the emergency backpack, assuming it would all get over in a couple of days. Now that I had plans to depart, I was unsure about my return.

So, the first thing I grabbed was my degree certificate besides a couple of other important documents. I took an extra pair of shirt and pants, stuffed them inside my bag along with a few necessary toiletries and gadgets. Then, I opened the bag of pet food kept in my cupboard and placed it where she would find them easily when hungry. My pet cat, Kitty, was smart and clever. She had always managed to find food by herself when I was away. Even though she was deaf, she was naughty and the cutest thing that had happened to me apart from my dog, Penny.

Penny was not as smart as Kitty. She was dependent on me for many things since she had been with me only for a month. I spotted her picture on one of my telegram groups where my friend had posted about selling her. She was so adorable that I was compelled to get her from my friend, who was returning to India. I contacted him and brought Penny to my home within a few days.

People usually say that cats are afraid of dogs. But in my case, it was the exact opposite. My dog was terrified of my cat. Her low purr would terrify Penny, but at times, she would muster her courage and manage to get into a paw fight with Kitty. However, sometimes Penny's aggressiveness would go out of the way, which is why leaving the two together on their own worried me the most. I knew they would get along and somehow manage to eat and survive till there is enough food at home. I petted them one last time before locking the doors, my hands unstable and my eyes filled with guilt and worry.

The remorse I felt for leaving my loved ones behind was immense, as I was unintentionally inflicting pain on those who couldn't even voice their fears.

As my steps moved farther away from my apartment's door, the purrs and barks kept fading in the distance. During the past few days, whenever I went away to the bunker, I wasn't this petrified about their well-being, as somehow, I thought this was a temporary phase, and I would always be there to look after them. So, after making the basic arrangements, I used to leave. But this time, it was as if both the pets had sensed that something was wrong and that I was moving away from them for a longer time, probably forever.

I tried to stay strong, but there was this tiny fear that kept scratching the walls of my heart. *'When all the food is over, what if my dog eats my cat?'*

CHAPTER – 12

"If we do not end war, war will end us."

— *HG Wells*

I thought, or rather, hoped that this war would be over in the next two to three days as the world leaders would take a step to stop the war and the loss. Assuring myself that everything would be back to normal soon, I went to the nearest subway. The people on the roads, who were usually quite organised and disciplined, and the subways that had fewer people on regular days, were now crammed with people, awaiting their one-way tickets out of Kyiv. Though the pain of leaving their home was more devastating than anything else, the Ukrainians had no other choice but to flee to save their own lives.

As I was walking, I heard the news of the Russian troops conquering the Chernobyl nuclear site and spreading their mark everywhere. It made the residents even more scared. After all, every person in the present generation would have definitely read about the nuclear bombing of Hiroshima and Nagasaki. None wished for history to repeat, that too, a gruesome and cruel one. Perhaps, if I had the strength of a marvel avenger, I'd be more than willing to be a human shield to the raining missiles and guns.

The Ukrainian army had lost many soldiers. So, the common people joined forces to compensate for the loss and protect their families. The citizens who stayed back in Ukraine, decided to give their best in the fight against Russia. A large group of men covered in puffed-up jackets and headscarves, walked behind the Ukrainian military tank in an attempt to stop the invading Russian troops. Along with the soldiers, these brave hearts stood in line to defend their nation. They may wear masks of strength, but they are not invincible. Even the nature's harshness reflecting in the snow was not as cold hearted as the ruthless attack on the innocent people.

As I walked down the street, I saw a couple; the guy was dressed in an army suit while the girl clung to him crying. A few kids surrounded him, wailing and yelling loudly, as they urged, "Papa, please don't leave us." "Dad, I'm scared." Their father patted the kids' heads, consoling them while tears brimmed in his own eyes.

So far, it was only the minor cuts here and there which life had thrown at me, but this was a gash right through my heart, ripping me apart. Someday, all of this would be a distant memory, just like the pages of a forgotten history textbook for the world. But for those who lived and survived the devastation, it would be a constant trauma; a constant threat looming over their heads, and a constant reminder of death and the uncertainties of tomorrow.

Russians would be reaching my current place in a very few hours. The news was spine-chilling. I didn't feel secure to be out in the open streets. Blasts were happening all around the country. One couldn't guess when or where the next blast would occur. No nook or corner of Kyiv was safe. The thought of it was like a demon clawing at the peace inside me. Though the home wasn't the ideal place to hide in the current situation, I still felt secure within the closed walls of my home.

I thought of taking my chance one last time and started walking from home towards the Demiivska subway station. When I was around 5 kms away from my home on my way to the station, the thought of returning home, and by some means, trying to stay safe within the confines of the walls, tempted me. Somehow, resisting the urge, I finally managed to squeeze my way into the subway, looking at the crowded platforms and the schedule of the upcoming trains. Though the chances looked slim to me, I knew that if I missed the opportunity now, I'd have next to no chance to escape. Soon, I was standing in the long queue, awaiting my turn.

The train that arrived then, was fully packed. So, we were asked to board the next train if it had any space for accommodating more people. I stood there waiting and kept praying for it to have some space. All the while, I was worried about my pets, whom I had left back at home, hoping for their safety. This reminded me of the instance when I was just as helpless.

***

It was a cold winter day. While I was taking a routine stroll, I came across a tiny black kitten, abandoned and on the verge of dying on the corner of the pavement. It looked quite fragile and its breathing was deep and slow. My heart went out to the little helpless being, and I immediately decided to take it with me. After I wrapped the black kitten in a towel, I took it to a vet, who did first aid. Luckily, I was able to save it. Like a mother feeding her newborn, I was bottle-feeding milk and giving medicines to the kitten.

There was a visible improvement in the next two days, as it was very energetic and even eating well. The cute eyes, soft tiny nose, and fur as soft and shiny as velvet had captivated me. I grew very fond of the kitten and made sure to do my best to raise it as a healthy cat. But my luck was not on my side. From the looks it gave me, I understood that it loved me too. On the third day, the kitten fell ill again. The eyes had turned gloomy and had a strange look. It was as if the kitten was grateful for being loved in its final moments. The thought broke my heart, and I couldn't bear to see the vulnerable creature in such a state.

In a desperate attempt to save the little life, I got into a cab, sat in the backseat and clutched the kitten safely in my arms while instructing the driver to rush to the vet. As its breathing turned laboured, I knew it was nearing its end. I did CPR multiple times and tried to revive it. Unfortunately, the feeble kitten took its last breath on my lap as my fingers lay on top of its chest. Tears flowed continuously from my eyes, feeling incapacitated for not being able to save the life. Gaining some composure, I informed the cab driver to drop me at a nearby park. I gave a proper burial to the little kitten and bid farewell to it, unable to overcome the grief. But when those doleful eyes resurfaced in my mind, I somehow consoled myself that I was able to make its final moments a happier one and that it didn't die alone.

As I exited the park, I decided to buy a cat from an adoption centre immediately. As soon as I entered, I fell in love at first sight with a white cat in a cage, having a lost look. Upon inquiring, I got to know that it had been abused by the previous owner. They had hit it with a stick, due to which the cat had lost its hearing ability. The after-effect of that trauma stayed with the poor thing. She used to get terrified if any person came near her. It took me some time to familiarise myself with the cat. Once it did, it became very playful and calm, and I realised how smart she was.

***

Finally, I got a subway from Demiivska Subway to Vokzalna railway station. Though my insides shrivelled as I left Kyiv, or to be precise, fled Kyiv, my second home, around three in the evening on 25 February, I knew I had no choice. Having no freedom to choose my next safety destination, I stood there, feeling vulnerable and lost. The only thing I knew was that anywhere else would be safer than staying here. I had no option but to leave it to destiny as I knew that the opportunity to escape may not come my way again. I was ready to board whatever train came next and wherever it took me. Luckily, I got on the next train to Lviv from Vokzalna, Kyiv.

CHAPTER – 13

"Violent statements and threats cannot provide a solution to the problem. They can only exacerbate feelings and make a clash of forces inevitable."

— *Stafford Cripps*

I barely managed to get on the train when the doors closed. It was so jam-packed that there wasn't even space to put a single foot. People sat on the passageway in between the seats, while a few managed to slightly rest their bodies on the available seats, and a few others were sitting on top of their luggage. As if my prayers were answered, I found a little place to sit down on the walkway, by the window. I looked out as the train slowly made its way out of the station, leaving behind a huge crowd waiting for their turn; a crowd that had aged people, ailing patients, non-resident students from other countries, and newborn babies, desperately waiting for their turn. Through the window of imagination, we glimpse worlds we can never touch, and sometimes, the view is more heart-wrenching than the closed doors we've left behind.

As the train started from the station, all the lights were turned off and it was pitch dark. We were instructed not to use mobile phones or any electrical gadgets and not to turn on the reading lights of the compartment. The windows too were shut for our own safety. In order to hide from the Russian spy drones and to stay out of the radar, we had to maintain silence and darkness.

News of drones detecting the trains and bombing them reached our ears, and we were all frightened and shocked to the core. Previously when we had a narrow escape from the invasion, we felt a bit relieved. But now the news of drone attacks made us wonder if we will make it through this time. The chances of us getting out of here alive seemed to be dubious to me now, as the glimmer of hope was quickly slipping away with each passing minute. The thought that the train would be detected and targeted, alarmed me. I shuddered thinking of the impact my death would have on my loved ones, in case I died. I tried my best and didn't have any regrets except the one decision I made — of leaving my pets behind. At the same time, I questioned myself if I had really lived my life. Perhaps, if I was given the opportunity to go back, I'd make sure to appreciate the little things and live my life to the fullest.

Meanwhile, the train kept moving forward but all the passengers inside were blind to the outside world. We didn't know where we were or what was happening outside. We wouldn't even know if there were any Russian tanks ahead of us. None of us had the exact information of the ongoing events. After going through such a traumatic experience, I couldn't help but have a deep gut feeling that some tragedy was waiting for us all. I kept praying and praying for the train to reach safely. Sometimes, I managed to switch on my phone and check the status in low brightness mode. The single bar signal that popped up for a few seconds displayed a few notifications on my phone, yet, my location was still unknown.

The journey that normally took a few hours now turned out to be unreasonably long, almost double the time. From the small talk, I came to know that the train was taking different routes, going through the interiors, to evade the Russians, as the main routes would probably be under their surveillance. Besides, due to lack of light, the train was going at a slow speed.

After a while, as the train continued its journey, the passengers started murmuring amongst themselves and looking around. Soon, the heat of a burning flame and the smell of destruction dissipated inside the cabin. When I peeped out of the window and gazed at a far distance, I saw fire unfolding its rage. As no one was there to cool down its wrath, it started spreading its wings. The reddish-orange reflection of the blazing fire on the clear lake nearby was akin to the orangish sky at sunset, dangerous and disastrous.

This disastrous reflection encroached on another beautiful memory of my trip to the Lake Lemuria near Lazurne, Ukraine.

***

Our university had given us a short vacation. Since all of us were free and had no plans, my friend and I planned a four-day trip to Lazurne along with his family. It was a fun and relaxing trip for us. The sight of windmills when we neared Lazurne brought a smile to my face. Soon, we reached our destination and settled down. The first thing my mind compelled me to do was to take a long walk on that land where the windmills were located. So, we set off on our way. The windmills were relaxing and fun to watch.

When I was a kid, I used to see huge white metal in the shape of a long conical ruler being carried in trucks on the highways. At that time, I used to think of them as parts of an aeroplane. I thought, maybe they were the tail fin or the wings of an aeroplane. Even then, I wondered about its unusual shape, which didn't fit the description of an aeroplane. Much later, as I grew up, I knew that those were the blades and the hubs of a windmill. Walking under the windmill, when I reminisced about it now, it all seemed funny. It's true that the innocence of childhood is what has kept humanity alive. It's necessary to keep the child in us alive, however old we may grow up to be.

We were excited to explore Lazurne, a beautiful resort city near the Black Sea with attractive lakes. On our first day, we went to the Black Sea for a swim. We took a long relaxing swim, rejuvenating ourselves in the water to our hearts' content and then rested on the sun loungers for a tan, enjoying the warm sun rays. The sight of the waves smoothly gliding against the sand and taking a bit along with it was soothing to watch; like a long-lost lover reuniting with his beloved, only to be pulled back again by the forces of nature. With every fleeting meeting, he took back a piece of her, bit by bit, gaining immense satisfaction of being with her.

The next day, we planned to visit the most beautiful lake near Lazurne, Lake Lemuria, which has a very high salt content. Though I was aware that the pink colour of the lake was because of the algae found in the lake, I was enraptured by the sheer beauty of it. The view was breathtaking. The water on one side was crystal clear and clean, making it a perfect spot for pictures. I clicked as many pictures as I could, wishing to capture the place so that it would always stay fresh in my memories, and then dove right into the water for a swim.

However, what intrigued me the most was the fact that it's impossible for a person to drown in this lake. I learnt that this was because of its high salt content, such that no matter how deep you go, you'll be pushed back up to the surface. This aspect was too tempting to resist. I had a crazy thought of testing this out and swam to the bottom of the lake. When I tried staying there for a while, I was pushed back to the surface. Soon, I was floating on the surface of the water. The experience blew my mind; I was as excited as a kid who had found the most ingenious toy. It felt like flying under the water. My friend and I, being the craziest ones, did this multiple times and ended up having the time of our lives when we experienced the thrill of being pushed up to the surface each time.

Somehow, I couldn't help comparing the different facets of life. When you feel like drowning in your misery and want to give up on life, you are pushed back to the surface to combat and fight for yourself.

On the third day, while we were walking around, we found a long and narrow strip of land in the water. The water level was up to the knees, and one had to walk to cross to the other side. In the narrow piece of land, the water levels were shallow when compared to either side, where the water was quite deep. It had a lot of varieties of fishes in a plethora of patterns and colours. Gingerly, I put one leg in front of the other, taking careful steps on the narrow bridge.

I spotted many jellyfish too while walking. Though they were very beautiful, I was scared of their poisonous bite. A little further, I began to enjoy the walk, watching all kinds of fishes and loving the feel of water till my knee. We crossed over to the other side and looked at the picturesque view. The Lemuria Lake is at the border of Kherson and Crimea. Standing near the border, I gazed at the other side and longed to travel across the border without the tedious visa process. How wonderful it would have been if we could explore different cultures and languages of different places without a visa! After all, I doubt that was how God had planned it. The borders were drawn by the greed of mankind.

On the last day, we again went to the beach and indulged in all the fun sports. They had many water sports to take part in. However, one such sport which grabbed our attention was a caterpillar-shaped airboat ride. We put our legs on either side of the boat and sat comfortably with our life jackets on. This airboat was pulled by a speedboat and took us deep into the sea. Once there, the boat took sudden turns, swayed, and slithered, exactly like a caterpillar, moving up and down along with the waves.

For half an hour, we were having fun on this bumpy ride. Then we played many other sports, ate food from the food stalls, and then sauntered on the beach, enjoying the salty breeze and the balmy weather. The evening was even more beautiful with the azure sky tainted with deep orangish red as the sun prepared to rest for the day. The reflection of these colours in the lake water made it gleam like liquid gold, making our eyes shine with contentment and happiness. Overall, the atmosphere of merriment prevailed, and we all had a ball of a time. With a lifetime of memories to cherish and smiles on our faces, we returned to Kyiv the next day.

***

The fume's reflection on the lake made me realise the stark difference between the joy that the reflection of colours brought me then and the pain and sorrow it inflicted now. Red, the colour of love, the colour of beauty, had lost its charm as it now depicted nothing but destruction and reminded me of the bleeding wounded people of my beloved country. It was like the two sides of the coin, the two sides of life.

CHAPTER – 14

"There is no glory in battle worth the blood it costs."

— *Dwight D Eisenhower*

I texted my friend in Kharkiv again, as I wished to check up on him. It was disappointing to know that he was still stuck there, and so were the other people. Residents had been staying in the bunkers for the past two days, safeguarding themselves and their loved ones. Sadly, it was the time of snowfall, which made the situation worse. Ukraine was like a snow globe of blazing fire. Due to the roadblocks, air attacks, and the approaching Russian troops, the officials too had a hard time finding a safer means of evacuation for the citizens. At the end of the second day since the attack, around sunset, the electricity and water supplies in Kharkiv were cut off.

Just as my friend had feared, the usage of the storage water cans was fast depleting the reserves and there was a water shortage. All the other emergency supplies too were on the verge of getting over. People had nowhere to go to fetch water. Like paupers, they had to share a slice of bread for a meal. The condition was desperate. So, when there was nil movement outside their building, people peeped out of their windows, scooped a handful and filled the bucket with snow and used the melted water for drinking and washing. One may consider it lucky that it was snowing but it was real hell. If it would have been the hot summer or spring, they would have been clueless about how to sustain themselves without water. The pictures he sent and the text he shared were like a million thorns to my heart. It was hard for me to control my tears and calm my aching heart. The darkness in the train couldn't hide the melancholy and distress of the people who were constantly praying or whispering among themselves, scared stiff.

The train was now passing by the factory which we had seen from afar. Smoke was rising high and the raging fire came into full view. The red flames were blazing and had consumed the entire building. Huge tanks and the steel base were the only things left, but it seemed as if they too would become prey to the fire's hunger. A few fresh blasts were occurring intermittently inside, possibly due to the left-over chemicals or the gasoline cans.

The darkness of the moonless night and the train corridors dissipated, owing to the burning fire that threatened to consume everything.

I shut my eyes and was thankful to have escaped from the grim situation that the entire country was facing, but the heat, the smoke, and the bloody visions will be etched in my memory forever till my last breath.

While facing situations where we were swaying between life and death, I couldn't help remembering the story of my grandparents who had faced a similar situation.

***

At the time of India-Pakistan partition, my great-grandfather, Mr Harichand Chopra, was with his family in the now-Pakistan-occupied province. He had a four-year-old son, my grandfather, Mr Shankar Lal Chopra. Since my grandfather was very young, he couldn't remember the incidents before he came to India. But the aftermath was imprinted deep in his memory. The violence had brutally robbed him of his innocence. The struggles my great-grandfather had to go through to start his family in an unknown land with nothing in his hands were as fresh as new in his memory. But his father, Mr Harichand, remembered every bit of the riot and chaos and used to narrate those stories to my grandfather. The trauma doesn't end once the violence does; it lasts forever in the minds of the sufferers who visualise those moments over and over again.

On the other hand, my mom's father, Dr Charanjeet Lal Malhotra, was thirteen years old at the time of partition. So, he too remembered most of what had happened. He used to live in a village called Kot Shakir, Sabbad Kaler, Zila Jhang, Tehsil Chiniot, which was located within walking distance from the Jhelum River. Their village and the neighbouring villages were all in arid land. Their lives were going on well and they led a happy and content life. It was the year 1947. For many days, talks about partition between Pakistan and India were going around, following which, many arguments and fights were going on in several parts of the country. However, they all prayed fervently that no such disaster would occur and matters would settle down over a period of time. Unfortunately, matters only worsened with each passing day, until one day, when they all came to know that the partition was inevitable. On the night of partition, riots broke out everywhere, and angry mobs were destroying everything.

Nonetheless, my grandfather still believed that it was temporary and things would be back to normal soon. Around midnight, they decided to go to the city, just as a precaution. He thought that they would go for a few days and then return. So, my great-grandfather took his family and left his home, after giving the keys to the neighbour. When he was halfway through while going to a nearby village, he saw a group of people rushing from the direction of the other village.

They asked him, "Where are you going? If you are thinking of going to that village, don't! Dacoits have attacked and have started looting the entire village. There is also an angry mob of Muslims fighting and burning down the whole place. So, don't go there. Go to a different village and try to save your lives."

Hence, he had to return to his village. Later in the night, the dacoits reached Kot Shakir and began ransacking the people. Another angry mob of Muslims, too, happened to be there. Everyone had to escape and find a safe spot for hiding. They were brutally killing the husbands and taking their wives away. The dacoits rode horses and were causing a ruckus. My grandpa was standing on the side of the path with his childhood friend and watching the scene with terror-filled eyes. He knew that if he wanted to save himself, he couldn't afford to lose his wit or courage. While the horses were standing on the centre pathway, he crouched down, hid from the dacoits and the Muslim mob, crawled from behind the horses, and quickly crossed the path to the opposite side.

To hide from the dacoits and the angry Muslim mob, he ran into one of the neighbour's homes, which happened to belong to a Muslim lady. Chaos had broken out by that time, and all the villagers were running in different directions. People didn't know what was happening and in which direction the other family member was running. The Muslim lady recognised the two kids. She quickly ushered them inside her house and hid them in a huge wheat storage barrel. Then, she took the Quran, sat in the front entrance room of her house, and started reading it. One of the men from the Muslim mob had seen my grandpa and his friend running into a house. So, they came to her door and asked, "We saw two Hindu kids running here. Where are they?"

She put her hand on the Quran and said, "I won't lie when I'm reading the Quran. They didn't come here. Don't worry. I promise. They might have run away in a different direction." The dacoits stared at her for a moment as if to ascertain and looked around the house. Feeling helpless, they left the house. When a lie is spoken for others' well-being, the intention supersedes right and wrong.

The dacoits were robbing the houses and killing many people while the angry Muslim mob was torturing the villagers and burning down the houses.

But as soon as they heard that the Sikh soldiers were coming to the village, they were petrified and ran away from there.

After both the gangs left, the Muslim lady brought the kids from the hiding place and handed them over to the families. My great-grandfather thanked her for her benevolence. He was always of the view that religious or political differences should not amount to a lack of compassion. And this was proved by the kind-hearted Muslim lady. He then went to check on the other people in the village. While looking at the other houses, he spotted one open house which had been looted. The daughter of that house had been taken away by the dacoits, while the father and mother were killed. The mother of that girl was found sitting in the kitchen corner. Looking at the *roti* burning to ashes and the blood sprayed across the walls, one could guess that she must have been attacked while cooking.

The sight of destruction all over the village was too terrifying to be expressed in words. Within no time, they decided to leave the place. They prepared a *tanga* to leave the village and go to a safer place. As their home was just 3 kms away from the nearby village, they decided to go there. Before leaving the house, they dug up a hole in the ground of their house and hid every valuable thing they had and left the place. Other people who had managed to save themselves from the dacoits were also with him. My great-grandmother was carrying a small pot during the journey. When they reached the Jhelum River, someone from the crowd noticed the utensil and shouted, "What are you carrying? We are here trying to save our lives and you are carrying such useless stuff."

She was too terrified to answer but then said hesitantly, "I… I am carrying the pot in case someone needs water to drink." However, they sneered and grabbed the vessel from her, threw it away, and shouted at her to save her life first. She helplessly looked at the vessel rolling away from her on the sand and falling into the waters of the Jhelum River. Sometimes, you see life slipping away from your fingers, just like the grains of sand, but you can do nothing about it.

All of them successfully managed to reach Jhang, from where Sikh soldiers took them in a truck to Lahore so that they could be sent safely to India. But what they heard from the people in Lahore scared them to the core. A train had gone to India from Pakistan with the people who were trying to get to safety. Sadly, angry mobsters had killed every single person on the train, such that the train had reached India, filled with dead bodies. In response to that, the same train was sent back to Pakistan from India carrying the same dead bodies. After hearing this incident, violence knew no bounds for days to come. Once triggered, brutality is hard to be controlled, as humans continue to act ruthless in the name of getting even with each other. The only way to end violence is by putting a stop to the destructive thoughts in your mind.

Just then, another batch of Sikh soldiers came in a truck, informed them about the riots and violence, and asked them to leave the country as soon as possible. A second train from India arrived and all the village members boarded that train from Pakistan. To their relief, nothing happened to the train which my grandpa and other people got into, and everyone reached India safely. When my grandpa left the village with his family, he thought it was for the time being and had left all their belongings in their home. They had run away with nothing but the single piece of clothing they wore. Till the time they got into the train, they were still under the illusion that it was temporary. It was only after reaching India, they realised that returning to their home would be impossible.

The realisation struck with a rude shock. The place they called home, was now a distant dream for them. It was in a different country now, and to go back to their own house, they would have to get a visa and a passport. Once they knew it was completely impossible, both my grandparents composed themselves, accepted their destiny, and started their lives from scratch. Those who stand tall in the face of adversities, are no less than warriors who have won the constant battle of life.

***

After hearing his story, I was inspired to write a book about him. I started investigating and researching about the village and the incidents that happened during that time. When I googled about the village, I came across a song *'Khan ghara de band vy khana by mujahid mansoor malangi'* which has a line *'Tere piche Kot Shakir chadeya'*. It was penned as a dedication by a writer from the same village, 'Kot Shakir'. When I researched about the village, I found out that it has historical importance, as the village has ruins of an 1800-year-old Hindu temple. While searching further, I came across a piece of interesting information about 'Malhotra', my grandpa's last name. I read that both the Malhotras and the Chopras are a caste that belonged to the Punjab Khatri Community. They are the previous generations, natives of Jhang, Multan, Peshawar, Lahore, and Eastern Punjab areas. So, this further confirmed that we were connected to the Jhang Jila as narrated by my grandfather.

While reading about the Jhelum River, I found that the village Kot Shakir was around 2 to 3 kms away from the Jhelum River. I also knew that this river continued to flow in Srinagar, Jammu and Kashmir, India, where the G20 Summit of 2023 was taking place. After reading so much about the place, I had a deep desire to visit the Jhelum River in Srinagar since visiting Kot Shakir wasn't possible. I wished to touch the waters of the river once in my life, to feel the essence of my ancestral home.

Sometimes, even the farthest connection with something that was once an integral part of your life, makes you feel at home. My grandparents used to call the Jhelum River as Jhelum Dariyah, which means a river basin in Punjabi-Saraiki. Previously known as Multani, Saraiki was the language and dialect of my ancestors. Since this river is seasonal and uneven, dams were not built. And because of that, floods were more common in the villages surrounding the river.

I remember bits and pieces from my memory that my mother's grandma used to dote on me. My mom has often told me how much she loved me and played with me. Even though she tried to live a normal life in a new land, the horrors of her past still haunted her and she would randomly break down crying, sitting by herself, recollecting and narrating stories about her past life in Kot Shakir. As I was not mature enough to understand or recall those narrations, my mom used to tell me again when I was a teen. Back then, they were merely stories for me. But now, when I came across the same thing, I felt her pain. It's easy to say you understand one's pain but it's difficult to feel the same.

People say that in this era of globalisation, all countries are diplomatic and war isn't possible. But history repeats itself. It is a strange loop that keeps coming back. After my grandparents, I am the one witnessing history repeat in a different way and a different nation. But the horrors and the trauma are the same, which will continue to haunt one till the last breath, even after one starts life afresh.

CHAPTER – 15

"War is delightful to those who have had no experience of it."

— Desiderius Erasmus

After sixteen hours of travelling by train, I reached Lviv around seven in the morning. My friend's apartment, where I decided to stay for the time being, was a fifteen-minute walk from the railway station. Destiny decided to play its horrible game on me, yet again. I came out of the station and rang up my mom to inform her of my well-being. I was still talking to her when I heard the first siren blaring. I immediately disconnected the call and sent her a text that I'd call her after reaching my room.

The sirens went silent for some time. So, I hurried towards my friend's apartment and slumped down on the cushion. Just then, warning sirens resounded in the streets of Lviv. Within moments, another siren boomed from the clouds above, along with the roaring jet engines. Terrified — that one word couldn't possibly express the shivers that I went through upon hearing the siren., Forcibly moving my legs, I ran to the nearby building's underground for shelter.

Around fifteen minutes later, the sirens stopped. I stood there, waiting for a while to be sure that it was safe to go out, to be sure that the sirens wouldn't start again. After a while, I trudged back to my room. The whole day was spent in either sleeping or running to the bunker while the sirens went on and off intermittently. I lost count of the numerous times I ran to the nearby shelter. At one point of time during the night, when the siren echoed again after a long gap, I was exhausted. I felt numb and had no desire to fight any more for my survival. All that I managed to do was push myself to go inside the bathroom and lock the doors tightly, ready to face whatever was written in my fate.

Terror, agony, fear, pain — a plethora of emotions overflowed my weak body. Numb and tired, my legs moved out of the bathroom of their own accord as the sirens went off after an hour of dread. I threw myself on the bed and dozed off to a restless sleep filled with nightmares.

The next morning, as I sat in the temporary apartment, I called my friends in Kyiv and enquired about the current situation. One of them told me that residents were still there in the East of Ukraine, where Russians were nearing. I switched on the television and saw the news channels broadcasting updates on the ongoing war. A few channels had organised debates that included well-known speakers, which was only meant to increase their ratings. Devastated at the heart-wrenching scenes and dead bodies and blasts being played in the background, I kept switching from one channel to the other.

My hand involuntarily stopped at one Russian channel that telecasted live scenes of an ongoing festival in Russia. People were laughing and seemed to be having a glorious time, dressing up in expensive outfits, dancing and playing, swaying to the loud tunes. The streets were filled with joyous people celebrating life, a few even intoxicated, while their country was oppressing and destroying another nation.

I always wonder how complicated a human is. Forgetfulness is a disease but a good one, they say. Indeed, people are forgetful and even neglectful. I wondered what would be going on in the minds of those people celebrating festivities. Were they happy and celebrating because their lives were safe? Were they joyous because the destruction didn't happen to them? Or were they celebrating the victory of killing and wrecking the lives of a once peaceful nation?

Those who lack empathy do not think twice before trampling over others' dreams. This was the only thought that raged in my mind as my eyes glared at the television screen while the people danced away to glory.

I gazed out of the window at the ancient European city, known for its beauty and historical importance. Much to my dismay, just like Kyiv, Lviv seemed to be nothing of what I remembered from my previous visits. The exuberance and the charm of the place got lost in the savageness of the humans.

I visited Lviv twice during my university days.

***

The first trip to Lviv was for a medical conference with Dr Mobeen Sayed during my second year. We all had expected Dr Najeeb to join us but due to some last-minute changes, he couldn't accompany us. He was very famous among medical students in our university. Instead of him, it was his younger brother who had joined us. Akash, Jaspreet, Haider, and Aman were my companions for the trip. We went directly to the venue and attended the seminars. While Akash, Jaspreet, and I were attending the meeting, Aman and Haider managed to sneak out and roam around the city.

In the breaks we got between the seminars, we three were searching for Aman and Haider, curious to know where they were. Finally, by evening, when the conference was over, we were given our certificates, got our badges signed, and came out. As soon as we did, we saw Aman and Haider waiting for us, laughing at us. In the little time we had left at night, we saw a few places and returned to our rooms.

The next morning, we took a shared bus back to Kyiv. There were around thirty people on the bus. As the driver knew only the local language, it was difficult for us to communicate with him. What's more, he was acting a bit high-handed too. When we were mid-way, the bus driver stopped for a refreshment break. Even before the bus could come to a complete halt, Haider rushed to the lavatory. Meanwhile, the other passengers ordered some food to eat as all were famished by then. We ordered many snacks, burgers, fries, and chips and waited for the food to be ready.

The food was about to be served in a few minutes when the weird driver came to us and informed that he was going to start the bus. We requested him to wait for two more minutes, but he growled, "You eat your food. We are leaving now."

Saying so, he sat on the bus and started the engine. With no other option, we had to leave all the ordered food, paid for it, asked the people over there to eat, and left for the bus. We returned to Kyiv in a foul mood and heavy hearts, thinking about the weird experience.

We planned our second trip, which was for three days. During the trip, we visited the famous cat café that had a lot of cats roaming around within the premises. When I came to know that the customers are allowed to play with the cats, being an animal lover, I was over-excited to visit.. Once we settled inside the café, many cats started running around my feet, jumping up on me and purring around my table. Their furs were so soft and velvety. I played with them and had a wonderful time. I wished to stay there for a bit longer, but I had to leave after a while.

Next, we went to Lviv's Handmade Chocolate shop which was well known for its hot chocolate drinks. I kept up with the unspoken tradition and got handmade chocolates from Lviv as a gift for others as well as myself.

I then walked around, looking at the historical scenic beauty. The buildings were of vintage European style, neatly maintained and perfectly designed. They were all old but looked as fresh as new. On either side of the road, quaint ancient-looking benches were placed on the pavements. If one was to click a picture to have a classic 80s black-and-white look, those spots would be the best.

Next, I went to Ratusha in Rynok Square which, is called the rat house. It was my wish to visit this place. Ratusha is at the city's centre, and from where we stood, we were able to see half of the city. Lion Hill was also another hilltop viewpoint, which had the most enticing view of the city. To reach up there, we had to walk a long way up the hill. It was worth the effort and exercise, as the view of the city from the top of the Lion Hill was enchanting. All the monuments, buildings, and roads were so organised and orderly built. It looked like beautiful blocks of Lego buildings in yellow, pink, and orange shades, giving a bygone vibe.

I then visited the other tourist attractions like the Lviv National Opera House, Fountain Ivasyk-Telesyk, St George's Cathedral, Bernardine Monastery, Taras Shevchenko Monument, and the Lviv Museum of the history of religion. The extensive excursion was tiring but more than worth it. With wonderful memories, I returned to Kyiv.

***

The present ten days in Lviv after my escape from Kyiv were nowhere cherishable like the previous ones; rather, I had a hard time, trying to keep myself calm and think about the situation pragmatically.

CHAPTER – 16

"War is like volcanoes. None knows how it starts. Once it explodes, the repercussions can't be controlled."

-Storymirror.com

I wasn't a tourist this time but a refugee. The last time I was here in Lviv, they were joyful times, whereas at present, the city was near a war zone. Though Lviv was not under the direct attack of Russia, it was still in the missile zone. It was also near the borders of the cities that were under attack. The news went on about all the destruction that was done so far. The sights and the impending attacks were getting too much for me. So, eventually, I switched off the television and decided to go out for a refreshing walk to see what was happening around.

The city seemed to be all right but it had lost its charm. The people were all in a sour mood trying to keep up their spirits. When I visited last time, the people were in a jubilant mood, engrossed in wonderful dances on the streets along with people playing guitars and other musical instruments. The streets of Lviv were a happening place to uplift your spirits. Alas! This time, the atmosphere was quite dull. People were trying their best to forget that there was an active invasion going on the other side of their country.

Camps were organised by volunteers to educate people about the dos and don'ts in case they were under a bomb attack. It was a two-hour programme, and I joined the camp to upgrade my knowledge. There were other volunteer centres, too, which helped people in arranging first aid kits, camouflage dresses, emergency medicines, and other necessities. There were medical camps as well, treating many refugees and other wounded people.

To the country that gave me so much, I had nothing to offer but my help. The knowledge I had gained in this land came in handy, and this was the least I could do to show my gratefulness. As a gesture of gratitude to the land that had given me so many wonderful memories and made me the man I'm now, I decided to volunteer in the medical camps and all the other camps that needed any help. However, my way to the campsite was not so smooth.

I sat outside for a while, scrolling through my WhatsApp groups to check updates on Kyiv. The video that played in front of me shook me to the core. I saw the most soul-shattering sights. My gut twisted in pain and churned up while my heart was beating so loudly that I could feel it thundering in my ears. I saw the dismembered body parts, an arm and a leg covered in charred dried blood lying between the trucks. Half of the body secured by the seat belt lay on the driver's seat, the head turned at the most uncomfortable angle. The sight made me want to scream in agony but all I could do was stare at it, unable to accept the callous behaviour. Maybe the driver of the car who had passengers filming the horrors, felt the same too, probably even worse, seeing it in front of his eyes. The video picked up pace as the driver speeded up the car and swiftly moved past the horrific sight.

Hardening my heart as a rock and swallowing the huge lump in my throat, I entered the camp. I saw many women and young girls who lent their hand in preparing food and camo suits for the warriors. Camps were set for nursing the wounded. Doctors and medical students worked day and night in helping the injured civilians and the wounded refugees. A few took charge of collecting the items that many kind hearts had donated.

The medical camp looked like boiling lava covered up with snow, waiting to burst through any moment. The entrance was filled with basic supplies along with medical kits, food, and water. But as I went in, I saw devastating sights, enough to break one's strength and spirit. It smelt of blood and medicines. People were sitting with blood-soaked clothes, having deep cuts and head injuries. Open-fractured legs and arms with bones popping out, swollen eyes and lips, broken noses and cut-off ears, half-burnt faces and burn injuries in many places — each one looked painful than the other. The doctors were going from one patient to the other, trying to ease them out of their miseries.

At the far end of the camp, a young boy with his head bandaged, sat on the floor, clutching his fighter doll tightly to his chest. He was wailing for his parents. From the whispers, I got to know that the parents had sacrificed their lives to save him. His plight made my eyes pool with tears, all the more because I was feeling helpless. But I kept a tight rein on my emotions as this wasn't the time to break down. Eventually, the boy seemed to be too tired to cry. His tears dried up and his throat seemed to be parched when he whimpered, asking for his mom. Another girl, too young to realise what was going on, ran from one bed to the other shouting 'mammaa', her legs spilling blood, tracing the path she took.

There was a granny who sat in tattered clothes, her swollen eyes covered in gauze. She kept mumbling incoherent words and clamped her hands together, begging us to take her somewhere safe. I lost count of the injured patients I treated and worked as swiftly as possible, while my heart absorbed every pain. Unable to take it any longer, I was on the verge of breaking down and decided to leave after treating a few more injuries. I lost my will completely, my threshold limit was broken, and tears cascaded endlessly. Just then, I came across a teenager.

Her arms were dislocated and multiple shards of glass pieces were piercing her feet. What struck my heart was not the wound, but her pale and numb face. She was too terrified to even cry, as the missiles had shattered her emotions. She had become numb to the physical injuries and sat still, neither drinking water nor eating food nor answering the questions of the doctors. It was too difficult to treat her. Though we managed to treat her physical injuries, the mental trauma she was in would take longer to treat. She was an example of many citizens suffering out there.

Though I had been mentally prepared to witness the most heart-wrenching sights, I was shocked to the core when I saw the scenes that unfolded in front of my eyes. On my way back home, I saw the news channels broadcasting videos of some parts of Kyiv. A long queue of army vans, ambulances, and police vans paraded slowly through the streets. On either side of the road, as the ambulances and police vans holding Ukraine's flag drove past, people paid their respects and showered their love and sincere condolences to the deceased army men and civilians alike by kneeling on one leg with heads bowed down. Though I couldn't join them to pay my respects, I prayed for the martyred brave souls to rest in peace. The brave hearts sacrificed their lives for the love of their motherland. Can love be any purer than that?

The pain and trauma of the injured people shattered my soul, such that it rendered me restless even after returning to the apartment. My mind whirled back to the phone call I received from an Indian family who was stuck near Sumi. It was surrounded by places that were already sieged by the Russians and the family was struggling to get to safety. One of my friends had shared my reference to help them out.

The terror their voices displayed shook me to the core. It was like adding more salt to a bleeding wound. In a frightened tone, the man asked me, "Please, save us. If you have any contacts in the embassy, please ask them to come to our rescue." I heard another female voice, sobbing, "Please do whatever you can. I have a small baby with me. You can take whatever money we have but please help us out of here."

It scarred me so much that I immediately fished out a couple of my contacts who were in organisations like WHO and Red Cross. They were providing food and medical attention to the needy. I got in touch with them and shared the details of the family, requesting to help that family. Luckily, they were able to reach the family and escorted them to Kyiv in one relief vehicle. Thereafter, I had no update on how they managed. Though the threat was still looming over Kyiv, there were better options to get to safety from Kyiv compared to Sumi.

Amidst this grief and terror, I was going through after the medical camp, thinking about this brought me a little relief. Though from afar, I had managed to help a family in need. Hope still sparked inside me, like a flickering candle in the dark.

CHAPTER – 17

"I know the horrors of war; no gains can compensate for the losses it brings."

— *Adolf Hitler*

A writer's soul is a furnace of emotion, where the fires of inspiration and despair meld, forging stories that resonate with the silent echoes of our hearts. For around a week, whenever my mind was not depressed or too fragile to handle the trauma, I helped in the camps and volunteer centres. I took a break and stayed at home but nothing helped to wane off the after-effects of the war. I didn't cook much at home and bought ready-to-eat food at grocery stores to help me sustain myself.

One day, when I was out in the grocery store shopping for food, sirens suddenly started blaring. Shock gripped my body, and I felt too frozen to move. Everything that was happening around felt like a movie scene. People abandoned their carts and bolted out to find safety bunkers. A few people brushed past me, and that's when I got to my senses and ran out of the shop.

I didn't know where safety bunkers were in the nearby area. So, I ran to the nearby building where everyone in the shop was rushing to. There were three to four bomb shelters in the basement of the nearby buildings. The bulbs were tiny and dimly lit, with very few chairs to sit on. The place was a little dusty. I found a small spot at the far end of the bunker and sat for around twenty minutes, thinking of the happenings. The place was filled with kids of varying ages, which made me value the pleasant childhood I had. Looking at their terrified faces, I worried for the kids of Ukraine. The kids were in their formative years, when they were supposed to learn new skills, enhance their knowledge, play, and form bonds with their friends. Instead, they were witnessing humanity at its worst, unsure of what lay ahead for them in the future. They were spending their childhood hiding for safety under the bunkers, and I couldn't imagine the trauma that would be imprinted in their mind.

While in the bunker, my gaze caught sight of a couple of writings scribbled on the walls. The words and the desperation that came through had an eerie similarity to the caves I had visited last year. Sitting in the corner, my mind reminisced about the two trips I took to Odessa and Bukovel.

***

Our pediatric teacher, Maya, was taking classes for us. She taught us how to examine the ailing kids and write reports. One of the kids had an amazing talent. The confidence and dexterity with which he performed the magical tricks with cards at such a young age astounded the onlookers. All the students in our class gathered around him to watch his magic show, engrossed in the way he conducted himself and the quick movement of his hands. Once his show was over, we got done with our reports and went to the teacher.

On that Thursday, Rishabh, Bhavya, and I went to the teacher after class and bluffed so that we could skip the next day's class. We informed her that we had some work out of the city and wouldn't be available to attend the class. She accepted our reports and gave us permission to take the day off. As soon as we were out of earshot, we gave each other high-fives on being able to pull this off without a glitch.

Our trip to Odessa began on 27 September 2018. It was a three-day trip, since the next two days were the weekend. We reached Odessa by the evening. The next morning, we all woke up fresh and ready for an exciting day. As soon as we gathered in the hotel lobby, we three posted a wonderful picture of ourselves on our Instagram handle with the caption 'Odessa Vibes'. Within minutes of posting, we received comments from our teacher, Maya. It is when we read 'wonderful', 'amazing' and 'have a good trip', that our jaws dropped and we realised that we had forgotten about Maya following us on Instagram! Gosh! We were caught, as we had applied for a leave, stating work excuse.

We three were startled for a few minutes and looked at each other's faces, wondering about the repercussions. But then, we burst out laughing at our stupid mistake. However, as the teacher was a friendly one, she too had let this matter slide.

While loitering around, we chanced upon a beach. The sight of the sparkling water, the crashing waves, and the merriment on the people's faces was so tempting that we took an impromptu decision to dive in. As we had no change of clothes, we bought a new set from a nearby shop, and then dove straight into the waters. We stayed in the water for three hours, and had the time of our lives, swimming, playing, splashing water on each other, and having fun.

We then went on a cruise which took us a bit deeper into the sea. There, we were able to see a swarm of jellyfish as we stood on the deck, gazing at the blue waters. As such, it was a smooth ride with no particular sighting. We had a great time, feeling the balmy breeze while having small talk and fun. On our way back, I noticed a cute little hand-made pen stand in a nearby shop, depicting the speciality of the place, and bought it as a souvenir.

Our next stop was at the gurdwara, which was hardly an hour's drive from the beach. It was one of the very few gurdwaras present in the country. We prayed there, feeling the positive vibes, and spent a little time out there. I felt so much at home and reminisced about the times when I used to occasionally visit the gurdwara in Panipat. The priest greeted us and told us to wait to receive the *prasad*. Then, he specially made hot *pakoras* for us to eat. He took very good care of us and treated us like his kids. We felt nostalgic and had a good time relishing the delicious *pakoras*. After that, we travelled back to the resort. At night, we spent some time at the beach, revelling in the sight of moonlit waters and the whiff of the salty breeze, while the illuminated shacks adorned the beach. Eventually, we returned to our rooms and called it a day.

We spent the next day at Arkadia beach, which was near the place where we stayed. The atmosphere at the beach caught on to us. We walked and played songs, enjoying the atmosphere. The memorable moments were captured by us, as we stood in the water, clicking iconic pictures in weird poses.

Our third day stop was at the catacombs, the ancient tunnels that served as the safety shelters for soldiers during world war time. Paris is well known for its catacombs and so is Odessa. There were many openings that connected several areas within the city.

These tunnels were previously made, and history has that people who ventured inside these tunnels, went missing. As these missing cases increased, the government blocked many tunnels. Only a few were left as tourist attractions. However, people weren't allowed to travel through these tunnels.

When we went inside the catacombs, we saw intricate carvings on the walls and also noticed some random scribblings. Well-like structures and statues were seen in different places. Ropes were hanging from the roofs. Many pieces of machinery that were used during the world war were strewn across the place. There was even a wooden classic chess set found inside one of the catacombs. We looked at every detail with interest, as the various objects gave us a glimpse of how people must have bid time while hiding here. With our minds loaded with questions, stories, and images of the place, we returned to our place.

That night, we roamed around, having random talks and clicking crazy pictures. It was on the third night that we took a train and returned to Kyiv.

The writings that I saw in these caves read 'We don't know if we will return or not'. They were scribbled by soldiers who used the caves to hide during the world war. This line tugged at my heart, as I felt like I was in the same situation at that time. The war had messed up our minds and terrified us to the extent that we didn't know whether we would be fortunate enough to open our eyes the next day or not.

Not wanting to harp on the current situation, in a moment, my mind drifted to the other trip I had enjoyed with my friends.

The second memorable trip was to Bukovel on 17 September 2020. We were a group of five friends who decided to go on the trip — Rishabh Vig, Rishabh Dhingra, Vrinda, Alka, and I. We had planned to rent a car for this journey.

Both the Rishabhs were responsible for taking the car from the rental garage. In the afternoon, they left to take the car. . Unfortunately, when they were on the way to pick up the girls, the tyres of the car got punctured. After a long struggle, the car was fixed, and we started our journey around six in the evening.

We played songs at an ear-splitting volume and sang along, all the way to Rivne. Both the Rishabhs took turns in driving. By the time we reached Rivne, it was night, so we went to rest in the hotel rooms.

The next morning, we went to the famous Tunnel of Love in Rivne. It was basically an industrial railway tunnel of around 5 kms that was surrounded by green arches of grass and creepers. We noticed a few couples walking in those tunnels, lost in each other.

That is when some girl from the nearby tourist group chuckled, "No wonder it is named the Tunnel of Love. And you know what? This tunnel appears different in all four seasons. It changes its colour every season and looks incredibly breathtaking. Just look around, guys! It's such a wonderful place for photography. Now I know why this unusual place is a romantic attraction for tourists." Everyone smiled, looking at her dreamy eyes and teased her about it.

She merely grinned and added, "Legend says that if lovers make a wish and kiss under the tunnel, and if their love is true, then their wish would come true." This caught my attention, and I mentally made a note to visit this place in future with my beloved.

We had a wonderful time out there, lost in the beauty of the exotic place. It was almost three in the afternoon by the time we left Rivne. and we reached Lviv, late in the evening.

There, we went to Ratusha, the rat house, from where the entire city had a magical view. We leisurely walked around the streets, chatting and making fun of each other. Throughout the way, Vig was repeating his signature dialogue. He always used to say, "Life consists of three important things." He would then cheekily add, "Do you want me to say again what it is? Of course, they are not the basic elements of the earth." His jokes would make us all laugh as he reiterated for the thousandth time what those three things were. As if I could ever forget his epic dialogue, he asked me to make a note of it and further added, "When you write a book about us, make sure you document my lines."

It was well-known amongst my friends that I always intended to write a book on how NRI students sustain themselves in a new place during their initial years. Little did I know that the circumstances may take a turn such that one day, I would be penning down about how a beautiful country got invaded and how not only the international students but also the citizens had to go through trauma which would leave an everlasting impact on their minds. At that time, I assured him that I would share his 'pearls of wisdom' in my book.

We went to Bukovel the next day and straightaway headed to the Voda Club. Famous for its outdoor swimming pool, affordable spas, different types of saunas, bar, restaurants, and gym, this place topped the chart on our must-visit places. What attracted us to the place were the fun activities like paddle boating, a floating aqua park, and an outdoor pool with thermal water. We were looking forward to chilling out as it was a perfect getaway spot with all kinds of amenities to spend the weekend. We spent a few hours swimming in the outdoor pool and took part in some fun activities.

After having a pleasant relaxing time and a hearty meal, we went to the hillside, which belonged to the Karpathian mountain ranges. It was exciting to go up the hill via cable cars, looking at the amazing mountain ranges from the top. The lush green expanse of the beautiful trees and the blue sky was breathtaking. The clear blue and the luscious green were a mesmerising colour combination. We went there solely to enjoy the sightseeing. Many tourists had come with their families and were having a little picnic spot. We rested there for a while enjoying the refreshing breeze and the spectacular view. Revelling in the company and the invigorating place, it was with much reluctance that we left to go back home. On the way, we played Hindi songs and had a relaxing time, laughing and cracking jokes.

***

Once the warning sirens went off, I returned to the grocery shop, picked up my things, and locked myself inside the apartment in Vulitsya Boikiivska. Within minutes, I started receiving one bad news after another. One of them was that the embassies were shifting their base from Lviv to another country. Those were the ones that had recently transferred from Kyiv due to the Russian invasion. This was a definite indication that something grave was going to happen very soon in Lviv too. There were no signs of normalcy either. There was nothing much to pack anyway. This pushed me to take a decision to leave Lviv in the first week of March.

I was blank about where to go. Romania, Hungary, Poland, and Slovakia were the options I had. But the borders of those countries were not easy to cross, as many people were waiting in long queues. Compared to the other countries, Slovakia's border was less crowded and was easier to cross. So, I took the few sets of clothes I had and left for Uzhhorod from Lviv by car on the night of 4 March. I met a couple of people who were also on their way to Slovakia. So, we decided to travel together.

We must have been about 5 kms away from the border, where the taxi dropped us off. On the isolated road, during the dark hours of the night, we walked alone on the highway to reach the border as there were no buses. The chilling sensations we felt running through our bodies were not only because of the cold weather but more so because we didn't know what would happen the next moment. One couldn't be too sure before reaching the destination. Our senses were all on high alert. While our legs tried to pick up as much pace as they could, our eyes kept darting around, scared, expecting someone to come rushing towards us any moment.

It was around midnight by the time we were near the border. All of a sudden, we were surrounded by patrol cars. It scared the daylights out of us, and we froze in our places. In a moment, they marched towards us and started vetting us, suspecting us to be spies. They scanned us thoroughly and checked all our bags and mobile phones. After approximately half an hour, they were convinced that we were fleeing the country to be in a safer place and allowed us to approach the border, which was around 2 to 3 kms from there. We reached the border around two and had to wait for a transit till three-thirty in the wee hours of the morning. We sat there shivering in the cold, despite the warm jackets that we were wearing. I made small talk with the soldiers there and stood by the campfire along with them. It helped me pass the waiting time, keep myself a bit warm, and take my mind away from the horrible memories and the fear of the unknown.

Finally, after hours of torturous wait, access through the borders was allowed. We got our approval, the documents were stamped with Schengen stamps, and we waited in a queue to cross the border. People were giving out food. One guy handed over a sandwich to me. Moments of my childhood, where I used to go with my family and often donate food or the necessary items for living at orphanages and old age homes, flashed across my mind.

I, too, tried my best to donate here while in the queue, but they refused to accept. I used to feel proud and had a sense of accomplishing something whenever we donated. But the moment I accepted the sandwich and my hands were on the receiving end, I felt all my pride, ego, and self-esteem shatter. I was left with nothing. This was the worst feeling I ever had in my entire life, the one I never wish to feel again.

CHAPTER – 18

"Only the dead have seen the end of war."

— *Plato*

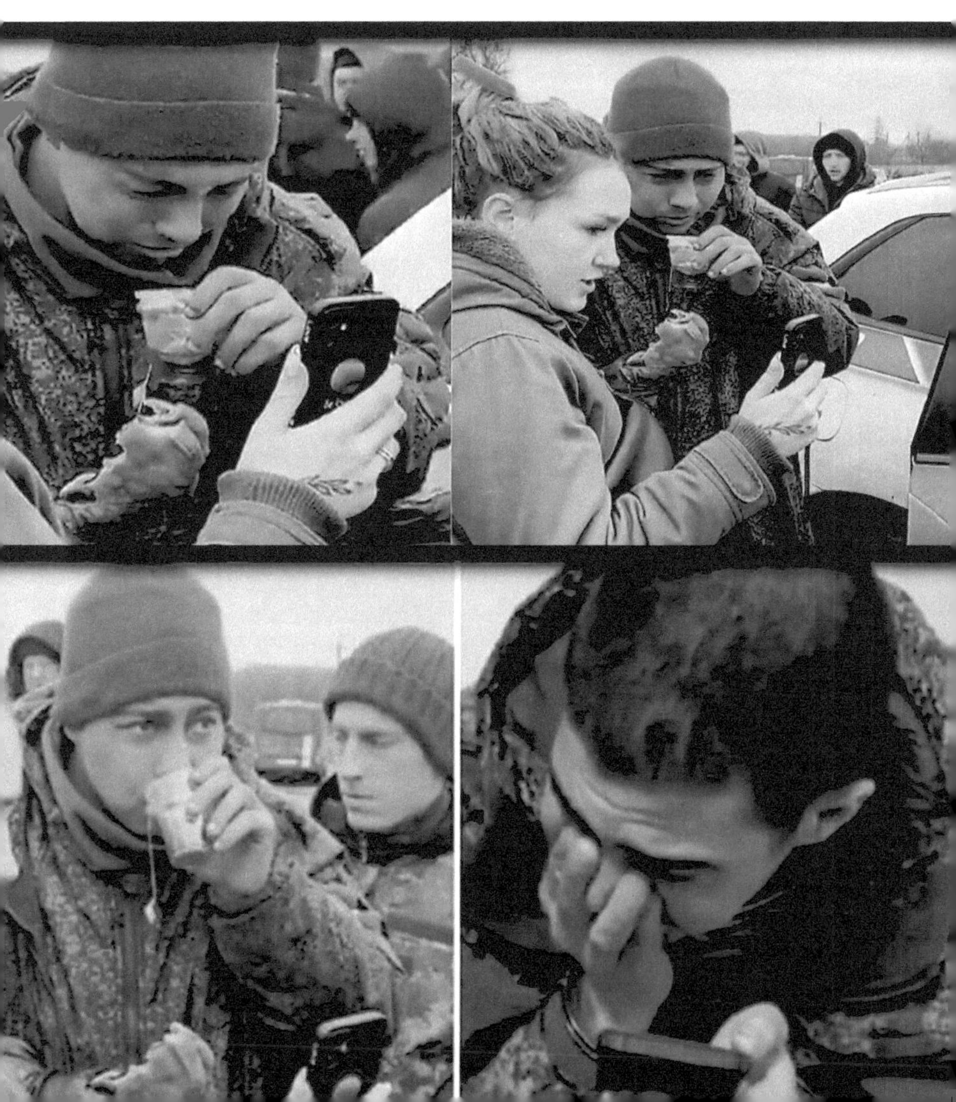

War made different people act differently. When I think back to the time when the Russian convoy entered the city, I had witnessed various mindsets of people. One group stood fearlessly, in front of the incoming troops, yelling that they would have to crush their bodies first before invading their homeland while the second group treated everyone as a human. They treated even the intruders as guests, providing them milk, pastries and homecooked food. This stumped the invaders just as much as the citizens who were ready to lose their lives for their country.

Once they were fed and content, a few posed a question to the Russian army, with due respect, "Why have you come here? What is the purpose of this attack?"

The young soldiers were so much moved that they broke down in front of the people who had shown them sympathy and love. Soon, they started pleading the women present there to lend their phones. They requesting them to call up their families back in their homeland so that they could talk with them. Many army men were equally shaken as the Ukrainians. The Russians had forced juveniles and young adults into this, hardly with any training much against their will. This unknown side of the Russian soldiers moved the soft-hearted Ukrainians.

My mind tried to process such hard feelings while I got on the bus to Košice. Looking back, I was relieved to have moved away from war, but at the same time, I felt a huge burden of memories crash into my chest. I was worried about how Ukraine, a nation without powerful weapons like Russia, would survive the war. The mere thought that Ukraine might fall, made my heart wince in pain. Even if they succeeded, we would be witnessing the aftermath of bloodshed and death. History has a weird way of repeating itself. It is while thumbing through those pages one needs to learn the art of survival. This was another lesson I learned, the hard way.

By God's grace and destiny's fate, I arrived at Košice safely on the morning of 5 March. I wasn't able to find an apartment till then, so my friend had referred me to Josefina, who would be helping me to find an accommodation. Mental and physical exhaustion took over me after the long night. I sat down staring at my foot while waiting for Josefina, who was kind enough to let us stay in her apartment for a while.

Flashes of blood, pungent stench, and dead bodies kept haunting me. Hunger and sleeplessness no longer seemed to be the issues. Though I had moved away safely, countless people had lost their lives, several were in a dire state, desperate to find a way out, the soldiers were facing the invasion with all their might, while my friends were still stuck back in Kyiv.

The war, which was the talk of the world, was at its peak. Reporters kept streaming videos and photos of the devastation. It was at this time, when I was in Slovak, the puzzle of the 64km long stalled Russian convoy on the outskirts of Kyiv was solved. Though it made me laugh, I felt pity too for the soldiers who were under the pressure to comply with the Government.

The convoy was stalled at the same place for nearly eight days with no signs of even a tiny movement, which had fed the hungry media world with ample of news to occupy themselves. Each came up with a theory of their own and danced as per the tunes of the country they favoured. Unrealistic plans to encroach Ukraine was imposed on the Russian military that lacked basic management and the plan to face logistical challenges as well as unanticipated weather conditions. It seemed as if they were stuck on the same spot exhausted of all their reserves, and reportedly falling short of fuel and food.

As per my acquaintances who were still in Ukraine, they were baffled as they had expected an aggressive attack. This was a mystery to the media too who were equally perplexed whether it was a planned stunt or a case of sheer mismanagement, more so because they had occupied the borders effortlessly. Many speculations were being circulated that the

Russian government was under the illusion that the Ukrainian government hadn't improved their intelligence system at all. However, that wasn't the case. I had personally known a sniper who was so skilled that each bullet he fired was sure to kill someone and there were ample skilled people who were being trained for the past couple of years, as they always had an inkling that someday, Russians would plan an attack on them.

The next thing that happened baffled me. It was kind of hilarious too when I think of it now. The Ukrainians used drones to gauge what exactly was going on. They had to confirm if the opponents were actually planning something big or if they were actually stuck. Ukrainians eventually realised that the Russians were waiting for supplies. Utilizing the opportunity, the Ukrainians attacked them from behind and when they did, the Russians were clueless and taken by surprise. They started running helter-skelter into the forest. This made me feel proud of the Ukrainians' intellect and at the same time, I pitied the Russians who were not as well-organised as they should have been.

On the other hand, my family and friends back in India were constantly checking on me, worried sick about my safety even though I was in Slovakia now. The first day when I had stepped into Kyiv, I had been loaded with dreams and ambitions besides the ample supplies. But while leaving, I could take only two sets of clothes. Though the luggage was meagre, my mind was brimming with the memories of Kyiv, both beautiful and traumatic.

Josefina's call broke my trance. She took me to her home, and we had breakfast together. She advised me to rest for a while, as later, we had to go for the registration work. She showed me the guest room and I was so grateful to her. Though her home was small and cosy, she managed to accommodate me in a small part of her house. The house felt warm and welcoming, just like her. Exhaustion took over me, and I fell into a restless slumber for an hour.

Later in the afternoon, after she returned from work, she accompanied me to complete the official registrations. She told me that she was trying to find a place for me to stay and assured me that I could stay with her till that time. Once I completed the legal process in the evening, I called her to pick me up. She showed me around, familiarising me with a few places. The warmth and kindness that the place and people displayed, helped me overcome the traumatic phase to some extent. I took in all the beauty while I could, too afraid it wouldn't last the next day. The endless days of torture had affected my mindset such that I still couldn't believe I had managed to escape the deathly experience.

By the time we reached her home, she informed me that she managed to find an apartment in Lake District, Nad Jazerom in Košice. The street address where we had to stay 'Dneperska 4, Nad Jazerom, Košice' reminded me of the Dnipro River in Kyiv, Ukraine.

Josefina remarked, "This is a very beautiful apartment near the lake. I studied in a nearby school and I'm sure you'll feel at home in that area."

I smiled and took my bag after which she dropped me off at the new apartment. It was empty and lonely, but I was thankful to have got a place to stay. Before leaving, she consoled me with her positive words, well aware of my inner trauma.

"You are safe now. Don't worry and sleep well," she further insisted, "Please don't stay at home and keep thinking about the same thing. I would suggest you walk around the place as it will help you to calm your mind. Get acquainted with the city and the people. I am sure it would refresh you," before closing the door.

To my astonishment, the city resembled Kyiv in numerous ways. The peace and beauty of the lake city were breathtaking. I didn't know if this was good fortune or a test of my life to stay at a place that was similar to mine back in Kyiv. As if the trauma I had been through wasn't enough, I was feeling homesick now. All the while, my heart was panicking and hoping that the upcoming days would be better. I wished for the war to end soon and hoped I'd return.

The waters were clear and fresh, carrying a soothing aura. The tall trees in front of the river and the greenery along the roads were refreshing. For a moment, I'd forgotten that I was in another country, running away from the war. I felt I was at home, safe and secure. I wish I were that capable of tricking my mind into believing the same. But the pangs I felt within jolted me out of my false cocoon.

The next day was a fresh start for me in the new city. The entire day was spent cleaning and making the apartment a good place to stay. I decided to follow Josefina's advice. Being lonely at home was a daunting aspect, anyway. So, I went for a small walk around the city. I spoke with a few people at the park and restaurants and listened to their experiences in this city. The people of Košice were very friendly and welcomed me warmly. They loved Košice so much and were affectionate and empathetic. Meeting them did help me divert my mind for a bit.

CHAPTER – 19

"Because I know war… because I know the horror, I don't want to add to it… After the war, we felt the need to celebrate life."

— Edouard Boubat

Over the days, the one thing I realised was that the Slovaks were the sweetest people one could ever come across. And this was reflected in the way they said *Dyakuyem,* which means 'thank you' in Slovak, in a sing-song manner with cheerful smiles on their faces.

The hospitality of the Slovaks moved me to tears. The government did everything possible to help the refugees overcome their trauma. They encouraged us to have a good time, go on trips, and not confine ourselves to our homes. And for this, they gave free passes for bus and train travelling so that commuting wouldn't be a hassle. The citizens, too, went out of their way and made it a point to not let us feel lonely. It was only on their relentless insistence that we would push ourselves to step out of home and mingle with others. I was so overwhelmed by the selfless love they showered on us that I couldn't be thankful enough to them. If at all I was able to put aside my thoughts for some time, it was only because of the compassion of the Slovaks.

Despite the numerous efforts of Slovaks, my heart and soul were still roped to Ukrainians. My fingers kept scrolling the newsfeed to know what was happening to them. I was dumbstruck and sat rooted in the same place, staring at the pictures that were floating on social media, where many lifeless bodies of men were laid on the grounds of Bucha, Ukraine, with their hands tied behind their backs. Few were stripped completely naked, while few were half-naked with eyes blindfolded. There were burn marks on a couple of bodies on the backs and stomachs, and the marks had an uncanny resemblance to the Swastika of the Nazis.

It became more heart-shattering and unbearable as I saw the naked bodies of women and young girls, hands and mouths tied with a thick band of cloth. By then, I was in a constant state of shock and depression. Each bestial incident shattered my soul further. Though my eyes were too dried up, like a desert that failed to sprout water, my heart still had the capacity to break into a zillion pieces, each of which was bleeding profusely. A symphony of screams and tears emanated from the depths of my soul, as if attempting to cleanse me of the very pain that weighed so heavily upon my heart. But write I must, for this pain is mine to articulate.

I was walking around the city on a random day when I came across Košice public library. I was looking through the bookshelves to pick up something interesting to read. While I was in one of the aisles, the librarian, Martina, stopped and enquired about me since I was new there. After talking for a while and relating quite a bit about what all I had endured so far, she looked visibly disturbed. Over the days, when I visited the library, she became very friendly. By then, I was used to people stopping by for a talk or helping me with something. While conversing with her, she discussed the trekking trips that she and her friends were planning. Though I was reluctant at first, I couldn't refuse when she insisted. So, I went along with Martina and other friends on many trekking trips. As expected, all those places were so lovely and refreshing.

We went for a hike along the path of Mengusovská dolina, a beautiful valley that led to

Popradské pleso lake. The hike trail was stony and we had to take careful steps throughout. We were out of our breath by the time we reached the Popradské pleso. The place was picturesquely brilliant. One cannot describe its beauty in words. The clear waters reflected the skies above and the majestic mountains nearby. The majority of the areas were filled with pine trees that added charm to the beauty. When I looked on one side of the lake, I was entranced by the ripples on the surface which were so even, with minute spaces between each ripple. The rocks along the shore were wonderfully moulded with green patches of algae covering a few parts.

There were tiny wooden bridges that connected the smaller divisions of the land. A stream of water cascaded down the path, occasionally crashing along the rocks. The dried trees, faded in yellow, matched the wooden blocks of the bridge. Behind an uneven row of dried shrubs and trees, stood the bright, strong, and tall greenery. Leaves of some trees were coloured bright red with a mixture of orange. The pleasing combination of bright and faded colours was soothing to my eye.

Crossing the smaller bridge, we went on to the other side of the lake. From here, we were able to view a larger area of the lake and the mountain.

We rested for a while on the shore, looking at the calm lake and clicked as many pictures as we could as a reminiscence of this mesmerising beauty. As we walked along the stretch of the lake, we found a stone bridge. It was a few feet above the water level and built from many rocks which seemed to be glued together, connecting the two halves of the land. It was as if the rocks were handpicked to match the background of the mountain and the flowing waters. The rock bridge's silver shine blended perfectly with the surrounding nature. Being a nature lover, I fell in love with this place. I was so enchanted by its elegance that I didn't have the heart to leave from there.

During the weekend, we roamed around the city. When we reached St Elizabeth's Cathedral at Košice's centre, Martina told me about an interesting tour guide to that Cathedral. He was a very funny guy. The way he guided the tour, and the tricks he came up with to make the tourists remember the facts of the place, was hilarious. I've never met such a humorous person in my life, who could make his work so enjoyable. He was spontaneous in coming up with funny jokes at the drop of a hat. He showed us around the cathedral. When we came to the front, he told us that he would be letting us in on a little secret about the place.

When the cathedral was built, the initial design was to build two identical tombs on either side of the building. They had completed building one of the tombs, but when they started the other, they were in shortage of funds for the construction. So, they had decided to finish off the other tomb at the height it was at. That was why one tomb looked smaller than the other. As he completed the narration, the expressions on his face made the whole group giggle. I wasn't sure if what he said was a fact or if he was bluffing to justify the short height of the other tomb.

We went up to the cathedral from where the entire town was visible. The roofs of the houses were visible in perfect order, whereas the big streets and the old roofs were astonishing to look at. Then we moved on to the next part, where an entire city was found under the cathedral.

In the olden days, it was said that the city had a low level. With time, the sand deposits took place, and the city's level rose higher. Later, when people were digging up the streets, they accidentally found an underground tunnel. When people went inside to see, there was an entire street under the main street. It was like two parallel dimensions that existed in the same place. The authorities took the place under their supervision and built an underground museum to protect and cherish the history. The entrance for this subway museum was located in front of the cathedral.

We were walking around when I spotted an ice cream parlour, Arthur Gelato, that was thronging with people. If I would have had any doubt about the taste and quality, the crowd ruled it out. I was excitedly waiting for my turn to try out that place's ice cream. Also, I loved the caption they had put in front of their shop, which was enough to lure a person to get an ice cream.

"You cannot buy happiness,

But you can buy ice cream."

It was these little moments, which brought a smile to my face during the worst phase of my life. I retired home for the day after having a good time and felt as if I had moved a step ahead in finding my footing back.

CHAPTER - 20

"Live life when you have it. Life is a splendid gift — there is nothing small about it."

— Florence Nightingale

In the days that followed, I observed that Slovaks were nature lovers and loved to go on trekking trips.

I got acquainted with another person, Marika, with whom I went on a trekking trip with a group of around twenty-five people to Slovak Paradise. True to its name, it was like a paradise on earth. The fields on the slopes were lush green while the mountains stood majestically, covered by cerulean blue clouds.

Then, out of the blue, snowfall started, though for a short time. The sight of the snowfall, which once used to make me dance with joy, gave me jitters. I started shaking, as all I could see was the snow soaked in blood.

***

The moment flashed in front of my eyes when I was in Kyiv. I had been scurrying away to the bunker as soon as the siren started. But the moment I stepped out of my building, I was greeted with a horrifying sight. The ground, which had been laden with fleecy white snow hours back, was now nowhere to be seen. Instead, a bed of deathly red snow with not a speck of white met my terrified eyes. I started panting, suddenly out of my breath while my feet seemed rooted to the ground. The horrific sight of the red snow embedded itself deeply in my eyes, refusing to go away. The sirens were blaring loudly and incessantly by then, but I couldn't summon the strength to move my feet towards the safety of the bunker. It was at that moment, that another person running by saw me standing there and pulled me along with him. For a moment, I had been lost as to what was happening and kept looking behind, unable to tear my gaze from the horrifying view.

***

I felt being shaken by my shoulders. This jolted me out of horrific reverie, while my senses made me realise, I was in Kosice now, and not Kyiv. I gulped water and tried to get a hold on myself. In their midst, I intended to bellow soundlessly, concealing the eruption of my inner volcano. To divert my mind, I looked out of the window, and to my relief, it had stopped snowing. Gradually, I tried to gain some semblance of normalcy as I gazed around and made small talk with the others. Marika showed me the brochure of Slovak Paradise, probably trying to take my mind off the tragedy. At last, the place worked its charm on me, and I went quiet as I kept staring at the lush green on the way, which soothed my senses.

Slovak Paradise, also called Slovenský raj in the local language, is at the top of the hill. We drove and reached a small clearing where we parked our car. There, we waited for half an hour for the jeep to reach us. Being on the hilltop, it wasn't possible to reach there by our car. They had specially designed off-roading jeep vehicles to take tourists from the parking area to the top of the mountain.

Not wanting to waste half an hour in waiting, we decided to look around. The online pictures couldn't capture the beauty of the place; it was spectacular. There was a lake and a few houses, along with farms. Small huts were built for the animals. They appeared to be cute little puppet houses on the large slope of lush green mountains. Soon, the jeep arrived and we hopped into it. After an hour, we reached our hotel at the top of the mountain. The view from up there was bewitching. The grass felt soft under our feet with fresh droplets of water making it sparkle. Geravy Hotel was the only hotel on top of the Geravy mountain, where Marika had booked our rooms. It had wooden finishing touches and the ambience was cosy and relaxing.

As far as my eyes could see, everything was green and refreshing. Outside the hotel, they had placed a small wooden dinner table. Beautiful flower beds adorned the corridors of the hotel rooms. Cows were grazing on the grass, and there was an energetic little dog that kept us company when we were chilling on the hotel lawn.

On the first day, we decided to trek in the mountains near the hotel area. The weather was quite chilly and the breeze was so cool. We wore our leather jackets and hiked up the mountains. We walked slowly, chatting along the way, and clicking profile worthy pictures of us having a great time.

Haze covered the lower areas as we went higher up the mountain. We reached the top and stood near the cliff looking down at the breath-taking view. It seemed surreal, as if we were floating on the clouds while we could catch glimpses of what lay beneath. From the top, we could see a small irregular oval-shaped lake. Many huts were built on the slopes of the mountains that were evenly spaced and appeared like blocks of a chocolate bar. Sitting on the edge of the cliff, we clicked pictures of the lake. The sight was so inviting that we climbed down the hill to have a closer look at the lake. After spending some time near the lake, we returned to the hotel.

The second day was when our actual journey to Slovak Paradise started. The Sucha Biela trail up the mountain was rugged and rocky. Though it was a bit dangerous and scary to hike up the trail, the scenic beauty lured us to enjoy the hike. The path was filled with ladders, footbridges, and rails. We had to place careful steps on the rocks and the ladder, as the rocks were slippery and wet in some places. Most of the path was covered with broken logs of wood and fallen branches.

It was fun though quite exerting to climb up the ladders and the slippery rocks. There were a few metal steps too that helped to have a firm footing. As we kept nearing the waterfalls, we could see little streams of water flowing between the rocks. But once we reached the waterfalls, all our fatigue vanished into thin air; the hike was absolutely worth it. Nature was at its best there. I would have been a fool to have missed this opportunity. Initially, when Marika asked me to join, I was not in a good mood and didn't wish to go anywhere. But after coming to the place, I thanked them for convincing me to join them for this hike. The only thing my mind kept reiterating was, 'Paradise truly lies in the Slovak Mountains.' We returned home after a refreshing and relaxing trip.

Then after a few days, we visited Jasovská Cave, which is millions of years old. The caves were stunning, and overall, the environment was pleasant. However, as soon as we stepped inside the caves, the temperature dipped. It was chilling, as if we were in an air-conditioned room. It took us an hour to see all the places inside the cave. The rock formations and the needle-like structures hanging from the roofs of the cave, the huge stalagmites, were quite mesmerising to watch. Gazing wide-eyed at the wonderment all around, I realised why this cave was considered to be a Slovak gem. I found it particularly interesting to see that the cave had narrow tunnels which led to the other parts of the cave. The view of the vast stretch of green grassy fields was magical when seen from within the cave.

We had to be extremely cautious while walking, making sure not to slip or hit our heads in the low-ceiling areas. A 600-year-old inscription was also found on the walls of the cave. After exploring the place for an hour, we went up the hills to see the picturesque view. The peaks of the hills were covered with pine trees, creating a fairy-tale image. The intricate designs and details bowled me over once again, proving how nature is always the best. It is only the humans who decide to cross swords with each other and destroy everything.

EPILOGUE

"The real and lasting victories are those of peace, and not of ear."

— *Ralph Waldo Emerson*

Today, while writing this book, I recollect a bit from the speech by Sadguru that I saw when I was in Košice, Slovakia. These are a few excerpts from what Sadguru said:

"All of us people, were we all thinking all these bombs are being kept for entertainment, for display of its artwork, what did you think?

One day it will be used!

It has to be used somewhere. The question is where and on whom?"

"We have no intent of stopping the wars, let's be clear about it. When it happens to us or when it happens close to us, we will cry. When it's happening somewhere else, it's drama."

"For about two years, two-and-a-half years, I attended a lot of international peace conferences. Then I saw for a whole lot of people, this conference-hopping itself is a profession - they're making a living out of it. I'm the only idiot sitting there, thinking we are working for world peace."

"When they're the head of state, they will do war; after they retire, they will talk peace."

"If there are no human beings on this planet, the world is peaceful, isn't it?"

Today, I feel it's high time we think about what he said in that speech. Should we think twice when we feel proud of the bombs that our country possesses? Or our enemy has? Is there anyone who is serious about peace, or is it just business? For, come to think of it, in the absence of wars, how would the ammunition be used? For those generating income from this, it would be a huge loss. So, does that imply that, at times, situations are 'created' or hyped, or persons and nations are instigated deliberately so that these ammunitions can be used, and ultimately, bring in profits?

Once when I was walking around on the streets of Kosice, talking to random people, I met a guy who was sitting on the park's bench. I was watching news updates about the situation in Kyiv. Voicing my thoughts aloud, I initiated a random talk with him. His answers left me speechless.

I asked him, "Why doesn't Ukraine give up this land? In that way, at least peace will be maintained and lives won't be lost."

Instead of replying, he smirked and counter-questioned me, "Why hasn't India given up on Kashmir till now?"

This perspective stumped me for a moment. Before I could reply, he continued, "What will India do, if tomorrow, Britain comes to India and claims it was their territory before, and that they are now here to re-occupy what was theirs long back?"

I was shocked and replied thoughtfully, "Of course, we will fight for our survival!"

He replied with a faint smile, "Exactly! That's what we are doing."

I was too stunned to speak further, as it dawned on me how deep this subject was. I wondered, 'If I, an Indian, who went to Ukraine to study, loved the place so much in the short span of time, how devoted and loving must the citizens of Ukraine be towards their birthplace!'

That night, thinking about the different perspectives and the discussion I had earlier in the evening, I retired to bed. While I lay on the bed, for some odd reason, Josefina's words, '*You are safe here… you are safe… safe… safe…*' kept echoing in my head. After a long time, I felt at peace with myself. It was a bit comforting knowing I was out of harm's way. At the same time, a disturbing question crossed my mind, '*Safe… until when?*' Before the demons of the past could trap me in their clutches, I ignored the question and fell asleep as tiredness took over. However, the peace was not for long as I thought.

In the middle of the night, I was startled awake by the roaring noise of a flying aircraft followed by loud alarms and sirens. The sounds evoked terror which I had not felt in a long time. I couldn't help wondering whether it was an indication of another raging war. Ever since I came to Slovakia, I assumed that I had escaped from the clutches of destruction. However, now I didn't know what to think. From what I could gauge, my flight to safety had begun yet again.

About The Author

Dr. Nitin Chopra, with a remarkable journey that bridges the worlds of literature and medicine, is a testament to the profound impact of words and healing. His deep-seated passion for both writing and sharing profound insights reflects a life where words and the art of healing take precedence. While his roots trace back to India, it was in Kyiv, Ukraine, during his formative years, that he honed his career.

Poetry, specially love for Hindustani poetry flows through his veins, a constant pursuit of mastery with each verse. Non-fiction may not have been his initial path, but it was the haunting experiences that compelled him to become an unexpected chronicler of horrors. "The Life of Tolka" emerged from one such nightmarish ordeal.

In 2016, he earned the prestigious title of 'Youngest Poet of India', a testament to his art of winning hearts through words. He also had the honor of being a keynote speaker at Pravasi Bhartiya Diwas in 2016 at the Embassy of India in Kyiv. This author's words have the power to inspire, heal, and transform, making his journey both professional and deeply emotional.

Connect with him

www.drnitinchopra.in

doctornitinchopra@gmail.com

www.instagram.com/Nitinchoprapoet

About The Author

Dr Niveditha Preeth is a published author, scribbling tales on the mental canvas and brewing stories from imagination's pot. She loves healing during the day and touching souls at night through her scalpel and pen. Navigating the worlds of medicine and prose simultaneously, she injects creativity into the veins of conventional storytelling.

Finding refuge in the inked words, she believes in spreading smiles through her profession as well as her passion. Books give her hope and replenish her soul. Her debut book 'Destined Desires' was released by PWO in 2021. Though poetry, horror, and fantasy stories are her forte, she has dived into non-fiction in the hope of paying her tributes to the innocent lives lost and the struggling survivors of the war.

Connect with her

https://www.instagram.com/niveditha_preeth

https://cascadingwordsblog.wordpress.com

Acknowledgements

Writing a memoir is a solitary endeavor, but it is not a solitary achievement. We would like to express our sincere gratitude to all the people who have played a role in bringing this book to life.

First and foremost, we are incredibly thankful to our families - Late Mr. Shankar Lal Chopra, Late Dr. Charanjeet Malhotra, Mrs. Kamlesh Chopra, Mrs. Vidya Malhotra, Mr. Anil Chopra, Mrs. Suman Chopra, Mr. Vijay Chopra, Mrs Kanta Chopra, Ruby Saluja, Kamna Tageja, Gaurav Chopra, Ish Chopra, Dr. Parveen Malhotra, Late Dr. J. Subash M.B.B.S., Late. Mrs. Kamalabaisubash, Mr. Jagadesh Subash, Mrs. Preeth Subash, Mr. Somaskandan for their unwavering love and support. They have always believed in us and pushed us to pursue our passion for writing. Their constant encouragement and understanding have been invaluable throughout this journey.

We extend our heartfelt appreciation to our mentor, Dr. Rohit and our friends who have provided us with continuous motivation and inspiration. Their belief in our abilities has been a driving force, and their willingness to lend an ear and offer constructive feedback has been instrumental in shaping this memoir. I, Dr. Nitin Chopra would personally like to thank Dr. Naveen Monga, Chetan Pawar, Dr. Haidar Ali, Sheetal Yadav, Dr. Akashdeep Gill, Dr. Jaspreet Gill, Dr. Rishabh Dhingra, Dr. Bhavya Behal, Dr. Nausheen Ansari, Dr. Deepanjali Yadav, Dr. Ranjana Saini, Dr. Yaseen Sheikh, Dr. Sangeetha, Dr. Mario Menchero Robles, Dr. Khaled Lutf, Dr. Ahmed Al Kuhali, Dr. Keneddy, Dr. Shubh Ankit Saini, Amninder Singh, Anastasiia Lemish, Martina Jesenska, Marika Mihalova, Jozka Polakovicova, Mankarn singh, Mayank Khurana, Mateusz Przygodzki, Igor Sobitskiy and Vlad Sobitskiy who played a major role in creating wonderful memories and being there in the toughest phase of my life.

We extend our gratitude to our editor, Ms. Janki Thakkar, whose keen eye for detail and unwavering commitment to excellence have helped transform our words into a polished manuscript. Your feedback and suggestions have immensely enhanced the quality of this memoir, and we are truly grateful for your expertise.

To the publishing professionals of team PWO who have worked tirelessly behind the scenes to bring this book to life, thank you for your expertise and commitment to excellence. From the editors who painstakingly combed through every line, to the designers who brought the cover to life, to the marketers who have tirelessly promoted the book, your dedication to your respective crafts has made this book shine. Your dedication, enthusiasm, and belief in our work have made this dream a reality. We are honored to be a part of such a talented and passionate team.

We are indebted to the countless authors who have inspired us with their words and storytelling prowess. Your books have transported us to different worlds, evoked our emotions, and sparked our imagination. Thank you for paving the way and showing us the power of storytelling.

We also wish to extend our appreciation to the beta readers and critique partners. Your feedback and constructive criticism have been invaluable in shaping this memoir into its final form. You have challenged us to dig deeper, to push the boundaries of our writing, and to strive for excellence. Thank you for your time, effort, and relentless dedication to helping us create the best possible manuscript.

We are indebted to our mentor and teachers who have shared their wisdom and knowledge with us. Your guidance and expertise have been instrumental in honing our skills and improving our craft. We are grateful for the lessons learned, the challenges posed, and the encouragement given. Your belief in our talent has bolstered our confidence and inspired us to keep pushing forward.

Last but certainly not least, we wish to express our gratitude to our readers. Your enthusiasm and support mean the world to us. Without your dedication, this memoir would simply be words on a page. It is your love for literature that drives us to continue writing and sharing our stories with the world.

Writing this memoir has been a labor of love and pain. We are truly humbled by the support and encouragement we have received along the way. To each and every person who has contributed to the creation of this memoir, big or small, we extend our heartfelt thanks.

Your support, belief, and contributions have made this book possible, and we are forever grateful for the incredible journey we have shared. Thank you all for being part of this incredible journey.

With sincere gratitude,

Dr.Nitin Chopra

Dr.Niveditha Preeth

www.ingramcontent.com/pod-product-compliance
Lightning Source LLC
LaVergne TN
LVHW042359190726
843493LV00005B/1060